100

GREAT
MINDSET CHANGING
IDEAS

Simon Maier

Marshall Cavendish
Business

Cover image from Shutterstock

This book is in memory of Peter Miller, artist

Reprinted 2019

Published by Marshall Cavendish Business
An imprint of Marshall Cavendish International

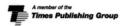

A member of the
Times Publishing Group

Other Marshall Cavendish Offices:
Marshall Cavendish Corporation, 99 White Plains Road, Tarrytown NY 10591-9001,
USA • Marshall Cavendish International (Thailand) Co Ltd, 253 Asoke, 12th Floor,
Sukhumvit 21 Road, Klongtoey Nua, Wattana, Bangkok 10110, Thailand • Marshall
Cavendish (Malaysia) Sdn Bhd, Times Subang, Lot 46, Subang Hi-Tech Industrial
Park, Batu Tiga, 40000 Shah Alam, Selangor Darul Ehsan, Malaysia.

National Library Board, Singapore Cataloguing in Publication Data

Names: Maier, Simon.
Title: 100 great mindset changing ideas / Simon Maier.
Description: Singapore : Marshall Cavendish Business, [2018]
Identifiers: OCN 1021826413 | 978-981-4779-72-2 (paperback)
Subjects: LCSH: Change (Psychology) | Attitude change. | Employees–Attitudes.
Classification: DDC 658.4094–dc23

Printed in Singapore

"Until one is committed, there is hesitancy,
the chance to draw back, always ineffectiveness.
Concerning all acts of initiative (and creation),
there is one elementary truth
the ignorance of which kills countless ideas and splendid plans:
that the moment one definitely commits oneself,
then Providence moves too.
All sorts of things occur to help one
that would never otherwise have occurred...
Whatever you can do or dream you can...
Begin it now."

– Joahann Wolfgang Von Goethe

CONTENTS

Chapter 4: Taking risks

Chapter 5: Be nice to you

Chapter 6: Attitude towards others

Chapter 7: Mindset at work

Chapter 8: Be Strong

Chapter Nine: Leadership

Chapter Ten: Develop and Grow

INTRODUCTION

There may be a number of bad things happening right now in your life, but odds are there are at least some that are good – and it's those that you need to embrace. You have choices. There are people in this world who have no choice at all. They have no options and no outlets for change. As terrifying as change and choice can be at times, can you imagine how terrifying it would be *not* to have the ability to choose?

A mindset is a mental attitude that predetermines a person's responses to (and interpretations of) situations. Essentially, our mindset determines our behaviour. The word 'mindset' is often used for a specific part of people's lives, as in 'the mindset of an entrepreneur', 'a winner's mindset' or 'an athlete's mindset'. Developing your mindset will help you learn, adopt new information, alter beliefs if necessary and help you act accordingly. Your belief-system is your mindset. Mindsets aren't comprised of any old beliefs of course. Firstly, they are yours – however you received or learned them. They manage your views, preferences and responses. And, sometimes, hates and extremes. One of the most powerful aspects of mindsets is how quickly they can be shifted (if you *want* them to shift) and how powerful the consequences can be.

In a fixed mindset, people believe that basic qualities such as their intelligence or talent, are absolute and unchangeable traits. They believe that what they have can't be developed and that innate talent alone creates success – without effort. With a growth mindset however, people's basic abilities can be developed through learning and effort; any innate talent is just the start, not the end result. Virtually all successful people have a growth mindset and believe that they can 'do' things and then find a way of doing them, sometimes well, sometimes not. But they try – and that's key.

There are signs to alert you when it might be time to make changes to your mindset. Maybe you're constantly focusing on what's wrong, rather than on what's right, in your life. Maybe you dwell on your disappointments and never think about the things that are going well. Maybe you're unhappy with what you are and with what you don't have. Perhaps you're a cynic and angry most of the time – particularly with those who are closest to you. And jealous of others. And perhaps you see yourself as a perpetual victim. Maybe you don't really believe in your ability to succeed and that any successes are all future failures in disguise.

Perhaps you don't want to face the truth. We can stomp about and moan all day about the rain which is stopping you playing golf, but doing that isn't going to make the sun shine. It's good to have a sense of justice, to appreciate how things *should* be, but perpetually complaining is a refusal to acknowledge the truth – which may not be changeable. There are simply some things you can't change, so let those be, plan accordingly and focus on those things that can be changed. You may wish that things were different or, more likely, that you wish that you had done something differently in the past. But, 'would', 'should' and 'could' are all 'wishing' words that add nothing to positivity and considering the past in a negative way is rarely helpful.

Sometimes you will undeniably believe that the world isn't fair. You may think that it's not right that something has occurred that is seemingly against you, perhaps (you think) making your life difficult or complicated. Well, the world isn't fair. Until you can accept that and change your mindset, your thinking will never be realistic and you will be plagued by resentment that your expectations aren't being met. Our expectations are a huge part of our mindsets. They are what we believe to be possible or necessary and set the platform for our experiences. If we have unrealistically high expectations, nothing will ever satisfy us. Maybe you're gifted and ambitious and, maybe, in a perfect world, you would have your first million by now. But we don't live in a perfect world and, with all the gifts and ambition that you may have at your disposal, you can't control every factor. But, you *can* set targets and you *can* meet – and maybe beat them. That leads to satisfaction and success and hopefully that's something that this book will help you better understand.

It's important to adjust our mindsets to survive and thrive in the real world. One person has some luck and you don't. You get a break and the other doesn't. All kinds of things are in action including chance, happenstance and circumstances, many of which you can't control. The important thing is to come to terms with what you want and what you *can* change to achieve what you want. You may feel dissatisfied and unhappy with everything you have (or don't have). But unhappiness must be balanced by the good things you do have – family, health, children, job, nice smile. The downside of ambition is that it blinds us to the wonderful things and people we already *do* have in our lives. Jealousies too drive us to dark places – often because of what we're taught to expect. We learn to want more. If we don't achieve what we think is due to us, that leads to dissatisfaction and that in turn leads to negativity. Certainly, there's always more for which to strive and that's a healthy part of ambition if 'more' means 'better'. The point is that all of us probably don't really appreciate what we already have (sometimes until it's gone).

Maybe you think that the world is against you – your boss, your colleagues, your family. Constantly viewing yourself as a victim doesn't empower you to change. Even if you were or are a victim, you need to overcome this low self-esteem by making a decision to reject that role and start creating a different one – something better – and that means a growth mindset. Perhaps you get involved with other people's opinions too often. Sometimes the negative mindset, with which you may find yourself struggling, reflects the messages you've received throughout your life from others. Maybe your parents told you that you shouldn't pursue your passions or maybe you had a negative partner who made you feel that you were never good enough. Perhaps a teacher said that you were rubbish. Maybe you listen to and accept idle gossip and particular credos. Maybe, in the age of digital news, you listen to too many conspiracy theories.

These scenarios are dangerous because they can, at their worst, lead to extremism. We can easily believe that what others say is true – whether it's about us or not. If it's about others, we often become transfixed with false information and we stop focusing on our progress. We begin to enjoy the theatre involving colleagues and possibly friends and family. Becoming too interested in other people's dramas is like a sport where we enjoy the scandal. It's not helpful.

Your mindset is a set of beliefs that should be constructive and helpful to you. If yours needs work, start now. Ensure that your beliefs become balanced. Think about your intelligence, your talents and your personality. Are these qualities simply fixed traits, carved in stone and that's that? Or are they things that you can develop or change? Such change is tough because our beliefs are often rooted in culture. Cultures are developed around behaviours, mores, religion, language, practices, diet, literature, relationships, art, morals and so on.

Today most experts agree that our mindset is not a result of nature *or* nurture, genes *or* environment. There's a constant give and take between each: the physical and the mental. In fact, as eminent American neuroscientist Gilbert Gottlieb put it, not only do genes and environment cooperate as we develop, but genes actually require input from the environment to work properly. That makes sense. Gottlieb's major contribution to the field of psychology was his theory that there is no predetermined path to development. That's an encouraging view because it means that any mindset can be altered. You have more capacity for life-long learning and development than you ever thought. We may start with different temperaments and aptitudes, but experience, training and effort take them forwards. Let's underline the word 'effort' without which nothing will change. And it's not always the people who *start* out the smartest who end up the smartest, depending on your definition of 'smart'.

It's one thing to have pundits offering opinions about scientific issues. It's quite another to understand how these views apply to you. Only you can determine if you become the person you want to be. Do people with a growth mindset believe that anyone can be anything, that anyone with proper motivation or education can become an Einstein or a Beethoven? No (or they shouldn't), but they frequently believe that a person's true potential is unknown (and unknowable), that it's hard to foresee what could be accomplished.

As a powerful adult, you have full authority and means to shift your mindset. And, in doing so, you can create the life or attitude that you want and need. A fixed mindset will cloud your judgment. You'll avoid challenges, you'll give up when things aren't going right and you'll think that you're not good enough at something. But, change *is* possible. The first step is to become aware of how your mindset is holding you back now. To change it isn't easy – but it's not hugely hard either and it's one of the most powerful things you can do. The very first step is to start.

CHAPTER 1
GET STARTED

1 SO, START

IF YOU DON'T ACTUALLY start something, then obviously nothing will change. So, until you begin your mindset change process, it won't alter and therefore neither will you.

The idea

Dropbox founder Drew Houston, who built a $10 billion company in his 20s, sees success and belief as one, "I've always found it valuable to ask myself, 'One year from now, two years from now, five years from now, what will I wish I had been learning today?'" He also points out that, "instead of getting ready, what you really want to do is get started."

Successful people commit to taking personal responsibility for their success. They set goals and do whatever it takes to achieve those goals. Generally speaking, each negative thought is a conscious decision to be miserable. There is no shortage of pessimists, critics and glass-half-empty people in the world. There will always be folk who can find the negative in any aspect of life; but there's no reason why we have to ascribe to their view.

W. Clement Stone, a mid-20th century American businessman and author is famous in part for this: "Aim for the moon. If you miss, you may hit a star." He was a huge believer in positive thinking and wrote: "There is little difference in people, but that little difference makes a big difference. The little difference is attitude. The big difference is whether it is positive or negative." After operating a small chain of convenience stores in southern California, Joe Coulombe had an idea: that upwardly mobile college grads might want something better than 7-11. So, he opened a tropical-themed market in Pasadena, stocked it with good wine and booze, hired good people, and paid them well. He added more locations near universities, then healthy foods, and that's how Trader Joe's got started. In Japan in 1917, a 23-year-old apprentice at the Osaka Electric Light Company with no formal education came up with an improved light socket. His boss wasn't interested so young Matsushita started making samples in his basement. He later expanded with battery-powered bicycle lamps and other electronic products. Matsushita Electric, as it was known until 2008 when the company officially changed its name to Panasonic, is now worth $66 billion.

Most of us want to make some changes in our lives. Whether it's to become fitter, work smarter or connect better with other people, we all want to change and improve *something* about ourselves. The problem is, the changes we want to make are never particularly easy and the results don't happen quickly. So, we try and we fail. And we don't try again. We say it didn't (or won't work). We may not be in control of everything that happens to us, but we *are* in control of how we respond to what happens. As we'll see, failure is often part of eventual success. People start in all sorts of ways but the key thing is to begin at all.

Melissa Galt, CreativeLive interior design founder tweets, "My advice is to find what lights you up, and do whatever it takes to make it happen." Richard Branson is a good example of someone who just 'began' with next to nothing. Branson epitomises the self-made entrepreneur. He started off creating a student magazine aged 16, then in 1970, he founded a mail-order record company – and within a year he had opened his first shop on London's Oxford Street – Virgin Records. Virgin has now become a brand which covers everything from telecommunications to space tourism. Jan Koum came to the U.S. from the Ukraine when he was 16. His family, struggling to make ends meet, lived on food stamps. In 2009, he and co-founder Brian Acton launched WhatsApp, a real-time messaging app with the aim of connecting people around the world. It essentially replaces text messaging and has 450 million global users, WhatsApp was bought by Facebook for $19 billion.

Sophia Amoruso is the founder of Nasty Gal and started by scouring the racks at second-hand stores and selling her vintage finds on eBay. She used the money from her sales to move her inventory into a warehouse and hire a few staff members. She used MySpace and other social media platforms to attract customers. And she eventually raised millions in investment in 2012, more than six years after founding the company.

Amazon's Jeff Bezos originally launched Amazon Auctions, to compete with eBay. That didn't go well so instead of sticking with the original idea, he stopped it, changed the model so that Amazon was started fresh as an outlet for third-party sellers. Li Ka-shing fled mainland China for Hong Kong in the 1940s, but his father died when he was 15, leaving the boy to support the family. In 1950, he started his own company with next to no money, Cheung Kong Industries, which manufactured plastics. The now diverse business is worth over $30 billion. Some people know what they want to do and focus on it relentlessly.

The practice

- If you want to make a positive change in your life, do it now. Start. Putting it off just gives you time to make excuses.

- Think about this: those with a growth mindset tend to have less stress and anxiety – and more self-esteem.

- Complaining about reality is not going to change it.

- Accept that the world will never ever be fair, as much as you might believe it should.

2 BELIEVE THAT YOU *CAN* CHANGE YOUR MINDSET

BELIEF THAT YOU CAN change is as important as starting the process. Believe in you. Think 'I can', not 'I might'. Think 'yes and', not 'no but'.

The idea

Enron's collapse was explained through its culture where praise for talent and intelligence led managers to lie about any problems rather than admit to mistakes so that the company could create a solution. No one wanted to admit to any failure because it was not acceptable in that organization's culture to make a mistake. A culture of growth mindset would have allowed for learning and solutions. In applying a growth mindset, it would have been better to promote a culture that accepted failure in order to learn. Stanford Business School professor, Jeffrey Pfeffer wrote that businesses often spend, "too much time in rank-and-yank mode, grading and evaluating people instead of developing their skills."

Neuroscience shows that our brains continue to develop and change. We can all learn. This is called neuroplasticity. Neural pathways are developed by doing or thinking particular things. The things that we do or say more often become hard-wired into our brains as habits. These form defined routes in our brains. Things become habitual and that's fine some of the time. But we can still change some habitual habits. The first step is to realise that we *need* to change or learn and then we have to *want* to change or learn.

Carol Dweck, Stanford professor who established mindset definitions writes that someone with a growth mindset, "thrives on challenge and sees failure, not as evidence of unintelligence, but as a heartening springboard for growth and for stretching our existing abilities." Embracing a growth mindset empowers the entrepreneur to be passionate about learning and exploring new possibilities. It also reinforces the fact that self and corporate belief is essential to success. Carol Dweck is quoted as saying, "The passion for stretching yourself and sticking to it, even (or especially) when it's not going well, is the hallmark of the growth mindset." Richard Branson writes, "I have always been keen to take calculated risks, and live with the consequences. All too often, talented people have fixed mindsets and are unwilling or unable to make the necessary changes to improve. When that happens, ideas stagnate, businesses stop growing, people stop learning."

Zappos (shoe retailer) is an interesting example of a business believing that it could change mindset development. Positivity there starts with new hires and a check to see if a cultural fit exists, which carries 50 per cent of whether a candidate is hired. New employees are offered a few thousand dollars to leave after the first week of training if they decide the job isn't for them. Ten core values are instilled in every team member. Budgets are dedicated to employee mindset growth. The business has established what the company culture is and fitting into that culture is the most important thing managers look for when hiring. This promotes the belief of 'can-do' (and self growth) which ultimately leads to happy customers.

The practice

- You have an internal dialogue with yourself every single day. Your mind is at work filling you with thoughts and ideas about what you're doing now, what you want to do and what you have done. Long-term memories, knowledge, facts, opinions and feelings are all stored. Pay attention to your inner dialogue.

- The good news is that you can change your mindset even if having a growth mindset doesn't come naturally to you.

- You're amazing. Believe it.

3 EXAMINE YOUR CURRENT MINDSET

GIVEN WHAT YOU'VE READ so far, think through what mindset you have and be absolutely honest with yourself.

The idea

There are several mindset types. The most common are 'fixed' and 'growth' as we've discussed. In a fixed mindset people believe that their basic qualities and abilities can't change. In a growth mindset, people believe that their most basic abilities can be developed. This latter view creates a love of learning and a resilience that is essential for accomplishment.

So, why wouldn't we want to change? Well, some people think that they can't. In order to change our lives, we must start by examining our own mental states: our beliefs, assumptions and expectations, the way we think the world is and the way we think that things should be. But we don't have to be trapped in old ways of thinking that undermine opportunity. For example, on a simple but often dramatic level, we don't have to take things personally or respond defensively to our perception of tone in, say, a text, tweet or email. We can also choose not to judge someone unfairly based on their appearance or religion alone. And we don't have to over-react to a situation and respond in a way that we may regret.

Changing beliefs starts by *challenging* beliefs. Once we start to doubt what we believe, change starts to become possible. A belief is simply a thought we've made real. It's not real, it just *feels* real – because we've been *told* it's real, because someone says it's real or because broadcasters and social media emphasise the 'reality'. Not easy? Correct.

The world's favourite ketchup maker, Henry J. Heinz, actually started out as a horseradish peddler. At the time, horseradish was a popular condiment, especially among English and German immigrants to the U.S. It was labour-intensive to make. Bottled horseradish existed, but the bottles were opaque and contents were easily cheated. Heinz felt restricted by what he was told he could achieve. Until someone told him that customers wanted to see what they were buying. So, thinking positively, he decided to package his offering in clear bottles. It was tough. In 1869, he formed Heinz Noble & Co. In 2013, Berkshire Hathaway and 3G Capital acquired H.J. Heinz Company for $28 billion.

It's nearly impossible to expand and grow, to learn, to take in new information and make new choices when we're confined to pre-existing and fixed ideas. If we want to work with others, we'll need to be able to accept (or at least understand) some of *their* beliefs and treat them with respect.

The practice

- Examine your current mindset by looking at your current belief-system, i.e. what you believe about everything: religion, sex, gender, money, ambition, learning, art, news, moral compass – everything. But you don't have to do this all in one go. You probably couldn't anyway. Small steps.

- Consider carefully what your mindset is. There may be a mix of positive and less positive thinking and beliefs. Try and sort out which is which. Write them down if it helps; be honest.

- As you go through your current beliefs, do you suspect that some of your beliefs may be misplaced or wrong?

COLLECT PROOF THAT COULD HELP YOU CHANGE

Changing anything needs reinforcement. With mindset change you need validation from others whose opinions (concerning your revised thinking) you respect. You need to read, listen and collect proof about any belief you're changing. Nobody else will do it for you and it won't just happen on its own.

The idea

We're surrounded by persuaders – advertisers, TV, politicians, religious leaders, social media – so it's hard sometimes to know how to change views and which. We also need proof of things to reinforce our thinking. Jim Stengel, formerly Global Marketing Officer at Procter & Gamble, acknowledged that proof and wide support for (in his case) products are essential for sales: "While many of P&G's products were very highly regarded for their functional qualities, some of our competitors had a stronger emotional bond with consumers' hearts. There was a lot of trust in our products, but there wasn't a lot of love."

Things of course aren't always black or white. There are people who will categorically state that the earth is still flat or, more seriously, that female circumcision is fine. Some of these beliefs are held in a cultural mindset and won't be shifted by any in that culture. Some are based on incorrect data. But they are believed.

You've probably held your big beliefs about life, money, religion, morals, politics, preferences and so on for a long time. Examine your mindset by looking at your current belief-system. Are these beliefs supporting you? Or are they limiting? You have to identify any blocks and turn them around. You can only do that if you get some proof and that means listening to a wider set of people whose opinions matter, by reading what leaders might say (although some of these too may have unhealthy bias), by reading balanced books and blogs and by talking to friends (but be cautious as to influence). Not everything is going to alter quickly (particularly anything that currently involves hate) and some beliefs may be impossible to shift easily.

PayPal wasn't founded to be the online payment service it is today. Founder Max Levchin maintains that PayPal was originally envisioned as a cryptography company and only later as a means of transmitting money. Only after several years of trial, error *and* proof of what could and wouldn't work (and overcoming user fraud that almost destroyed the company), did PayPal become the default online payment system. At various points in its development, the company considered changing business models. Each time it gathered substantial proof as to the way forward. Ultimately, flexibility and proof were major assets. Founded in 1998, PayPal was swift enough to change course in time to go public in 2002 and later was bought by eBay for $1.5 billion.

Google was once an unprofitable company, trying to find a stable revenue source. After making marginally profitable forays into selling search appliances to businesses and its own search technology to other search engines, it radically changed course because it found proof of a better direction. In 2003, the company launched its AdWords programme which allowed businesses to advertise to people searching for things on Google.com. Google took the leap from popular search tool to advertising powerhouse. In 2008, Google made $21 billion in advertising-driven revenue. AdWords comprises the lion's share of Google's total revenue and profits but wouldn't have existed had not the business challenged beliefs, gathered proof and established that it was right for a market on a big scale.

By challenging beliefs, it simply means finding ways to doubt the beliefs that we want to change: What caused me to believe this in the first place? Why? Where did I learn this? Is it valid now? Does this belief hold true in every situation? For everyone? Anywhere? Always? What are the exceptions to this belief? Who holds it whom I admire? Why? The answers to questions like these help us to see that the belief isn't perhaps as solid as we thought it was. At some point violent people stop having the ability to feel empathy for others and it may be nigh on impossible to change a belief that keeps them violent. When societies are involved in long-term, intractable conflicts, individuals tend to develop highly polarized views about how to resolve them, which can make it even harder to reach agreements. But we have to assume that beliefs can be changed and not everybody is radical or extreme.

Proof in business is essential. Sometimes it's market research. Avalanche Energy in the U.S. developed a new way to collect solar energy that didn't involve photovoltaic cells. Their device was the size of a satellite dish. Their potential niche – i.e. anyone who paid an energy bill – was massive. Their breakthrough, after performing customer research to get proof, was to fine-tune their offering. They recognized that the specific problem they could solve for customers was saving them money on their home hot water heating bills. So, they positioned their product as an easy-to-install roof-based device that worked with existing hot water tanks. They did this, even though their product had the potential to generate electricity, using a slim micro-turbine. The reason? They'd discovered it was easier to get homeowners to buy upwards on a simpler, more affordable initial investment. They gathered proof to change people's minds.

The world has a great history of having inaccurate opinions. For example, few saw the financial crash of 2007 coming or that Brexit would occur or that Trump would be president. Microsoft famously predicted that Apple wouldn't gain a sizeable share in the mobile phone sector. Challenging beliefs is all about trying to work out the truth. Or a *different* truth. When we change an opinion or belief that is held fast by our cultural group at home or work then, when we voice it, the results may be tough. We may become ostracized, laughed at or threatened. You may want to keep your own counsel, but you can't always. If you want to change, you will.

The practice

- Question whether a current belief is helpful to you or not.

- As you examine each of your beliefs, consider this: a statement without proof is at best an opinion. Opinions can be wrong or less than totally correct.

- Is there any weight and credibility to justify either current or new beliefs? Have you had a negative thought about a belief since childhood and never challenged it? Why? Can you do it now?

- If there is no proof, then any thought or, rather, belief, is just a guess, a speculative hunch. In reality, it's more likely to be a misplaced myth rather than an accurate assessment of your current situation.

TAKE TIME TO WORK OUT WHAT YOU *REALLY* WANT

WE OFTEN HAVE VAGUE ideas of where or what we want to be. In order to make a good mindset change, you do need to think about, and then target, what you really want to achieve and that 'want' needs to be specific, not vague. It also needs to be realistic. Yes, it can be a stretch, but must be possible.

The idea

In a 2016 interview, Denise Morrison, CEO of Campbell's Soups said, "I knew I wanted to run a company. I knew that as a young person. So, everything that I did was about getting the experience and the skills to be able to do that, not only to get the job, but do it really, really well."

We are not clear sometimes of what we want until we achieve fame and then we think we want more of that. But that's a loose target. When leaders or indeed any achievers focus on external gratification instead of inner satisfaction, they lose the original reason and motivation for their success. They surround themselves with sycophants who tell them what they want to hear. Over time, they are unable to engage in honest dialogue and others learn not to confront them with reality.

In June 2005, Steve Jobs gave a commencement speech to Stanford's graduating class: "You've got to find what you love…. The only way to do great work is to love what you do. If you haven't found it yet, keep looking and don't settle." We do need to know what we want and it has to be precise – and achievable, otherwise we drift. When we think negatively about what we *haven't* accomplished, we must take time to think if we really want those things. Finding out what's important to us can help eliminate both what is *less* important, what is unimportant and what might be regarded as bad.

In 1950, Tony Maglica moved from his war-torn home in Croatia to America. With little English, he settled in Los Angeles and took jobs wherever he could find them. In 1955, after saving $125, Tony put a down-payment on his first lathe. He started working in a garage – determined to produce flashlights for which there was a growing demand. He focused. Today, Maglite is the standard issue flashlight for most police officers worldwide.

In 2016, Mary Barra, CEO of General Motors was determined, "If we win the hearts and minds of employees, we're going to have better business success." Brian Chesky, co-founder and CEO of Airbnb wrote, "If you want to create a great product, just focus on one person. Make that person have the most amazing experience ever."

The practice

- There's no value in aiming for something that's totally impossible, despite what anyone may say. You probably can't achieve everything that you want in life. Few of us can. Focus on the most important and achievable thing/s. Give *that* your full effort.

- Don't think you have to follow the path others dictate if in your heart you know what you want to do.

- However, do consider other people in your decision-making if you know that they can support your thinking.

- If all you think about is what you don't have, then you'll perpetuate your lack of what you don't have.

- Choose to think more positively about what your future can hold and what you're capable of. Understand that the past is a reflection of what you thought and believed and how you acted *in the past*.

GO FOR MARGINAL GAINS

MARGINAL GAINS ARE CONCERNED with small incremental improvements in any process, which, when added together, make a significant overall improvement. They help us make progress by taking small steps – on the basis that, over time, each tiny increase will add up to an overall gain enabling us to achieve and win.

The idea

In 2010, British cycling as a sport was very low. No British cyclist had ever won the Tour de France but, as the new General Manager and Performance Director for Team Sky (Great Britain's professional cycling team), Dave Brailsford had to change that. He believed in the 'aggregation of marginal gains.' He explained it as "the one per cent margin for improvement in everything you do." He believed that, if the team improved every area related to cycling by just one per cent, then those small gains would add up to remarkable improvement. His team started by optimising the things we might expect: nutrition, weekly training programmes, bike ergonomics. They also searched for one per cent improvements in areas that were overlooked by everyone else, such as discovering the pillow for each cyclist that offered the best sleep, testing for the most effective type of massage gel and teaching riders the best way to wash their hands to avoid infection. They searched for one per cent improvements everywhere – in meals, in TV viewing, in energy drinks and so on.

Brailsford believed that Team Sky would be in a position to win the Tour de France in five years – by 2015. He was wrong. They won it in two years (2012). Team Sky rider Bradley Wiggins became the first British cyclist to win the Tour de France. That same year, Brailsford coached the British cycling team for the 2012 Olympic Games and won 70 per cent of the gold medals. In 2013, Team Sky won the Tour de France again, this time with rider Chris Froome who, incidentally, won it for the fourth time in 2017.

Mercedes F1 Team Director, Toto Wolf said in 2017, "We are maxed out on performance... and when that happens everything becomes more marginal". While other teams are playing catch-up to recover from design mistakes (forced upon them trying to catch Mercedes), Mercedes is making further gains in every aero, mechanical and human component and process from helmet design to fruit juice.

It's so easy to overestimate the importance of one defining moment and underestimate the value of making better decisions on a daily basis. Almost every habit that we have – good or bad – is the result of many small decisions over time. We forget this and convince ourselves that change is only meaningful if there is some large, visible outcome associated with it. We often put pressure on ourselves to make some earth-shattering improvement that everyone will notice. Meanwhile, improving by just one per cent isn't notable (and sometimes it isn't even *noticeable*). But it can be just as meaningful, especially in the long run. Each weakness in a process may not be a threat, but provides an opportunity to adapt and create marginal gains. Rapidly, they accumulate.

Many of the most innovative companies are now using a marginal gains approach. Google, for example, runs 12,000 data-driven experiments annually in order to discover small weaknesses and, therefore an opportunity to make small improvements. One found that by tweaking the shade of the Google toolbar from a darker to a lighter blue, it increased the number of click-throughs. This marginal change increased revenue dramatically.

The Practice
- Focus on doing a few small things really well. Once we do this, aggregating the gains we make will become part of a bigger impact.

- Look at your list of ambitions and reassess it. What's at the top? Ask yourself again whether it's actually achievable. Can you manage this goal?

- Most change is gradual and it's easy to overestimate the importance of one defining moment and underestimate the value of making better decisions on a daily basis.

- There is sometimes power in small wins and slow gains.

KEEP FOCUSED;
STAY ON TRACK

SOMEONE SAID, "IF YOU chase two rabbits, both will escape." Keeping your goals in sight is tough, but obviously key to growth. Composer and lyricist Irving Berlin wrote, "The toughest thing about success is that you've got to keep on being a success. Talent is only a starting point in this business. You've got to keep on working that talent."

The idea

Ralph Waldo Emerson wrote, "Concentration is the secret of strengths in politics, in war, in trade, in short in all management of human affairs."

And author Jack Canfield, wrote, "Successful people maintain a positive focus in life no matter what is going on around them. They stay focused on their past successes rather than their past failures, and on the next action steps they need to take to get them closer to the fulfilment of their goals rather than all the other distractions that life presents to them."

It's interesting that many people can't say what the focus is of the business in which they work. We go to Amazon to buy something, to Google to search for something, to Facebook to connect with friends, to Groupon for daily deals, back to Amazon to buy stuff fast and to Twitter to send and read tweets. Setting goals helps to focus our attention and that in turn helps us to organize our resources to get what we want to do. By setting clearly defined goals, we can measure and take pride in the achievement of those goals. We can see progress in what might previously have seemed a long pointless effort.

Amazon's Jeff Bezos personally uses the reverse engineering process to formulate a focused plan. He establishes his end goal and then works backwards, until he knows exactly what it is he needs to do today. Nissan's CEO, Carlos Ghosn wrote of perpetual focus: "I know exactly where I'm going to be, what I'm going to be doing for the next 15 months. It's not only for me; it's mainly for the people working for me. They know when I'm going to be in Tokyo, when I'm going to be in Paris, when I'm going to be in New York – so they can organize themselves." Upwork CEO, Stephane Kasriel, says, "A few of the things people focus on every day are just not that important. You can completely eliminate those things."

The British Olympic cyclists developed a 'Podium Programme' during the Beijing and London Olympic games. That meant that they aimed for gold medals – nothing less. Our focus must be on clear markers of success. We have to know when we've succeeded. Abraham Lincoln's greatest inspiration came from an intransigent belief that he had one focus only. Lincoln was certain his purpose was to preserve the greatest democracy the world had ever known and to ensure its "government of the people, by the people, for the people, shall not perish from the earth." And this was a man who was demoted in the army, managed a failed business and lost presidential elections eight times.

In 2004, Shell was facing an oil reserves crisis that ruined its share price. The then new group chairman, Jeroen van der Veer believed that, to survive, the corporation had to transform its structure. A series of global processes were identified. These, if introduced, would impact 80 operating units. While the changes were vital for survival, they proved unpopular as some countries stood to lose market share. The message was tough. However, for a change programme of this scale to be successful, everyone had to stick to the plan 100 per cent. It worked and many of its principles and focus are still used today.

In 2008, Santander wanted to establish a stronghold in the UK banking sector and acquired a portfolio of UK financial institutions. In unifying them under one brand, Santander aimed to turn them into a strong retail bank. To do this, a fast-track, systems-led banking model was needed to bring clarity, efficiency and best practice to all parts of the new business. For incoming Santander UK CEO António Horta-Osório, his focus would be to ensure that all stakeholders grasped the value of shedding 'old ways' and embracing the new – revolution, rather than evolution. In January 2010, Santander UK was launched. By 2013, it had become one of the leading retail banks.

If we try to change anything and fail, we've just proven one of the sturdiest truths of mindset change: failing at least once is part of the process. To focus, we all need positive reasons for taking on the challenge and imagining what it will be like when we get there.

The practice

- Once you know that your mindset change programme is working, stick to it.

- If you're lacking in a basic skill that you need to achieve your objective, get that skill.

- If you need help, seek it.

- Goals are set on a number of levels. First, you decide what you want to achieve. Second, you break the objectives down into smaller aims that you must achieve to reach your overall goal.

- The British Cycling Team had a motto: 'This is our focus. This is the line. The line between winning and losing. Between failure and success. Between good and great. Between dreaming and believing. Between convention and innovation. Between head and heart. It is a fine line. It challenges everything we do. And we ride it every day.'

DON'T EXPECT CHANGE TO BE EASY, BUT EXPECT IT TO BE POSSIBLE

BENJAMIN FRANKLIN WROTE, "WHEN you're finished changing, you're finished." Change is perpetual. It isn't always hard, but then it's not always easy. To make mindset change sustainable, determination to change is a must and you have to keep in mind that what you want to do *is possible*. So, expect to achieve.

The idea

It is possible to change and, having made up our minds to achieve something, we can. But we must be careful. Cynicism is a self-fulfilling prophecy. We have no chance if we assume that we have no chance. We can't allow opposition to let us lose our confidence and encourage us to adopt a negative attitude. Things may get in our way but let's see them as temporary.

Change is only successful when we believe, really believe, that we can achieve tangible results. That makes the possibility – and probability – of successful change a 'must do' and 'must deliver.' Following the 2008 financial crisis, UK-based RBS Group was ordered to sell its insurance business by European Union regulators, as a condition of RBS receiving £45 billion in a government bail-out. RBS's insurance business, led by Paul Geddes, was tasked with quickly separating its operations from RBS Group into a standalone company, in order to be ready for either sale or stock market listing. The management team turned the opportunity into a positive exercise and used the separation process to create a viable, standalone, rebranded insurance organization – Direct Line Group. It took only 18 months (and that is quick) to separate out every single strand of the business, from customer data, to independent functions and governance. After separation, the focus was on creating a new brand. In 2012 the company went for a highly successful IPO.

It's easy to get discouraged when we try and then don't get the results for which we were hoping. But the reality is that just making the effort is, in fact, progress. Change is not normally an event with an exact start and stop point; it's a process. Even if we take a few steps back, it's not tragic. In fact, change rarely occurs in a linear sequence and, when people falter, they usually don't fall all the way back to where they first began. In fact, if used correctly, the bumps in the road can serve as learning opportunities. In the 1980s, PepsiCo was aggressively targeting Coca-Cola causing Coca-Cola to re-evaluate its offerings. A sweeter drink was made by Coca-Cola called New Coke. The public didn't like it. Management decided to pull New Coke and replace it with the established formula and called it Coca-Cola Classic. Market dominance was maintained. To compete and to be seen as a responsible brand, it also needed to get into the healthier food and drink markets. Coca-Cola now sells more than 500 brands to customers in over 200 countries. Many of its products – like DASANI, vitaminwater and Evian – are considered healthy.

The Practice

- Change is a process, not an event.

- Change is hard and there are likely to be periods of relapse. But that's probably a) necessary and b) can be motivational.

- You will succeed if your change is rooted in positive thinking as opposed to guilt, fear, apology or regret.

- Spend time with others who are positive role models for the change you're trying to make or are involved in absorbing.

- Feeling overwhelmed by trying to change a behaviour tends to foster all-or-nothing thinking which won't end well, so just change in small steps albeit as fast as is necessary.

- Trying to take on multiple behaviours at once is a surefire way to drive them all into a ditch.

BELIEVE THAT YOU *WILL* SUCCEED

BELIEF IS WHAT YOU'RE fighting for in mindset change and your belief in changing or amending your beliefs is a given – or should be. Seeing success as the end-game of any initiative is essential and that vision must be clear to you. Blurred and vague visions don't work.

The idea

John F. Kennedy set out a belief in his country's ability to succeed when he said, for example, in 1960, "'We will put a man on the moon by the end of the decade." He created a clear objective and a specific time frame in which to achieve it.

Eleanor Roosevelt understood belief. She once said, "A good leader inspires people to have confidence in the leader, a great leader inspires people to have confidence in themselves." Mark Cuban, owner of the NBA's Dallas Mavericks, sold his company, Broadcast.com, to Yahoo for $5.9 billion. He admitted he was terrible at his early jobs – carpentry, cooking, waiting tables. He wrote, "I've learned that it doesn't matter how many times you failed. You only have to be right once. I tried to sell powdered milk. I was an idiot lots of times and I learned from them all. I believed in me."

Michael Jordan was left out of his school basketball team. He turned out to be the greatest basketball player and always had belief in himself. He said, "I have missed more than 9,000 shots in my career. I have lost almost 300 games. On 26 occasions, I have been entrusted to take the game's winning shot and I missed. I have failed over and over and over again in my life. And that is why I succeed."

Avoiding arrogance, there's nothing like believing in ourselves to create a successful reality. We must give ourselves the benefit of the doubt and believe that we'll succeed. Often, we don't realise how much we subconsciously harbour negative thoughts. A negative frame of mind often occurs because we won't let go of negative beliefs – and that includes thinking that we can't succeed. Sometimes self-pity adds to the negativity. As does fear of change. We have to *believe* that we can succeed. We might see someone else achieve success and feel that we're not able to do the same. Well, the simple fact is, we can. It's not enough to just say, "Oh, just think it will happen and it will happen." That's not the same as belief. There's also effort, want, need, aims and objectives. The point is, mindset alteration requires hard work and that work needs to be sustained. One of the richest men in Asia and a dominant figure in Hong Kong's economy, Li Ka-Shing started a business as a teenager en route to a $21 billion empire. By the age of 15 he had left school and worked in a plastics factory. He then became a salesman, outsold everybody else and became the factory's general manager by 19. In 1950, he started his own business and did almost everything all by himself. He puts it all down to focus and belief.

The practice

- Most things you have in your life are a result of your belief in yourself.

- Visualize what it is that you want to achieve. Think about exactly what your life would look like if you had already achieved your dream.

- Always act in a way that is consistent with where you want to go.

- The truth is that most of us have been conditioned throughout our lives to doubt ourselves. We must retrain ourselves to get rid of our fears and self-doubt in order to build self-esteem and self-confidence. Not arrogance.

10 CREATE *REALISTIC* GOALS

MANY PEOPLE START WITH unrealistic goals when changing their mindset. Don't.

The idea

Ben & Jerry's goal is to make the best possible ice cream. Wikipedia's goal is to help people to 'Imagine a world in which every single person is given free access to the sum of all human knowledge.' Disney's is 'To make people happy.' Coca-Cola aims to 'Refresh the world.' Amazon wants to be: 'Earth's most customer-centric company, where customers can find and discover anything they might want to buy online.'

Goals, for businesses and any of us, can be pointless if they're not realistic and very simple. And true. Mindset development necessitates ambition, but realistic ambition. It's hard enough to make changes in our lives and accomplish what we want, but if our goals are unrealistic, or not well-defined, then we're starting out with a handicap.

If we just think about a goal, it's not physically real – and it's easy for us to change our minds. The most important benefit of setting goals isn't only achieving them; it's the person we become in order to achieve the goal that's the lasting benefit.

Brit Morin, CEO and co-founder of Brit+Co (a site that 'inspires, educates and entertains real women with a creative spirit') left Google at 25 to launch her own company. On her site, there's lifestyle advice on everything from tech gadgets to makeup tutorials. She says, "I'm a visual person by nature so it's important for me to visualize my goals first, not just write them down in a check-list. Whether it's creating a mood board or flipping through magazines for inspiration, visualizing my goals actually motivates me to set a game plan... I make sure that my goals are actually achievable. Don't be overly ambitious, be realistic when setting goals... I also make sure that I set thoughtful goals that check the boxes: will this help improve my life and why is this important to me? You need to understand the value and importance in the goals you create and set in order to ensure you stick with them."

We all need powerful, long-range goals to help us get past short-term obstacles. Fortunately, the more powerful and realistic our goals are, the more we'll be able to act on and guarantee that they will happen.

The practice

- You may decide that you want to turn your life around and set out to accomplish a laundry list of goals at once. Don't. Because you can't.

- If you don't make time for your goals, you'll never accomplish them. Set goals that you realistically can achieve but, importantly, pick goals you want to achieve, not just because you feel you should.

- In goal-setting, be precise and avoid generalities. Wanting to be happier or a better person are noble things for which to strive, but hard to define.

- Ambiguous goals produce ambiguous results. Incomplete goals produce incomplete futures. Always set goals that are measurable.

CHAPTER 2
THINGS THAT GET IN THE WAY

11 DON'T MAKE EXCUSES

WITH ANY CHANGE, IT'S easy to make excuses either not to start, to stop or to reduce effort. These won't help you deliver. Excuses are a justification for failure.

The idea

Excuses make people feel better about themselves for not achieving goals but satisfaction is very short-lived when it's clear that excuses haven't changed the situation. We must think solutions not excuses.

People – managers, CEOs, politicians – offer every excuse in the book for failure: a bad economy, market turbulence, a weak yen, terrorism, hundred-year floods, storms, competitive subterfuge, digital interference – forces, in other words, outside their control. There are extremes: businesses go out with a big bang (like Enron). Others linger (like AT&T). Some fizzle out (like Polaroid). Failure is part of the natural cycle of business. But excuses aren't helpful. Reasons are better and solutions better yet. Some of the world's largest companies have lost at least two-thirds of their market value over time, including Hewlett-Packard, Charles Schwab, Cisco, AT&T, AOL Time Warner and Gap. Each came out with a litany of excuses. Jim Collins, author of *Built to Last and Good to Great*, says, "The key sign – the litmus test – is whether you begin to explain away the brutal facts rather than to confront the brutal facts head-on."

If we want to change, then we must reframe our mindset. If we want to reframe our mindset, that involves change. Often, when we initiate change, we think about all the things we *should* be doing – but we forget to stop the habits we *shouldn't* be doing – and they become a set of excuses. We respond to circumstances because we're provoked or frustrated. We often react instinctively, which leads to a negative action or reaction, but we can switch our mindset to one where we respond thoughtfully, rather than instinctively.

When we reframe our mindset from reacting to responding, we're in control. We're not in control of everything that happens to us, but we *are* totally in control of how we *respond* to what happens to us. "That's not my fault," is a common excuse and not one you should use. The best leaders take responsibility for their actions. As Henry Ford advised, "Don't find fault, find a remedy."

Saying "Don't bring me any bad news" doesn't make the bad news go away. Positive people want to know (maybe the first to know if they're managers) about the issues that need immediate attention. As Former U.S. Secretary of State Colin Powell said, "Bad news isn't wine. It doesn't improve with age." Excuses stop us doing things. They become reasons for 'running away' or 'stopping'. Excuses are rationalizations that we make to ourselves (and then to others) about people, events and circumstances, things we set out to do, things we know that we need to do. They are usually invented reasons created to defend our behaviour or as a means of negating accountability.

Living a life of excuses can have very serious consequences. Not only will excuses prevent us from reaching our full potential, but they will also hold us back from recognizing opportunities, talents and skills that we may have which can help us grow. Making excuses can also lead to: massive regret, self-limiting beliefs, pessimism, paranoia, mental blocks stifling activity or creativity and pretence that issues don't exist.

The practice

- Ask yourself why you want to make an excuse.

- If you're frightened of failure, think about what success will look and feel like.

- Maybe you're worried about success because success carries with it the 'burden' of repeating it. That's OK. That's also why you are in the process of changing.

- A big fear is that of making mistakes. We all make mistakes.

- To overcome your excuses, you must first admit that you're making them in the first place.

REMOVE THE 'I CAN'T' DEVIL FROM YOUR SHOULDER

OFTEN, WE HAVE A little devil on our shoulder telling us to do the wrong thing, to do nothing or that we can't do something. We have to fight this 'can't' devil. In the process of mindset change, you have to keep and stay positive.

The idea

Fred Astaire failed his first screen test. The MGM casting director noted that Astaire, "Can't act. Can't sing. Slightly bald. Can dance a little." Astaire, incredibly positive, went on to become a hugely successful actor, singer and dancer. Author Stephen King was penniless when he was first trying to write. He lived in a caravan with his wife and they both had several jobs. He received sixty rejections before selling his first short story, *The Glass Floor* for $35.

We have to avoid anyone telling us that we're going to fail unless it's obvious that we are. We have to avoid doubt unless there's a very solid reason for doubt. We have to avoid 'can't' unless we really, really can't.

Anthony Robbins, life coach and known for his seminars on becoming a 'can do' person', wrote that fear and the phrase 'I can't' are nothing more than what he calls False Evidence Appearing Real. It's our perspective of fear that frightens us and prevents us from effecting change. However, once we gain understanding about the things we fear, that's the moment we build enough confidence to move forward towards the attainment of our goals. If we say, 'I can't do it', maybe we don't want to whatever 'it' is. 'Can't' is not helpful.

The practice

- By saying you can't do something, you're already doubting yourself, submitting to defeat and making that barrier around your existing mindset tighter.

- How you approach an opportunity and the result of it is solely based on and down to *you*.

- Persist, persevere and resist the temptation to give-in to 'I can't' thinking.

- If planning is all you do, then this indicates that there might be fears that are preventing you from actually *doing* anything.

- Making comparisons between yourself and others will often make you feel disheartened.

- Just because you didn't finish or achieve something before doesn't mean that you're not able to now.

13 DISMISS ANYTHING NEGATIVE

FRENCH PHILOSOPHER, MICHEL DE Montaigne, wrote, "My life has been full of terrible misfortunes, most of which never happened". Negativity is an obvious barrier to change. Don't let negative thoughts overwhelm you when you're feeling low or when you feel that your journey towards a growth mindset is slow or has been derailed a little.

The idea

Ford's Former CEO, Alan Mulally, said, "conveying the idea that there is always a way forward – is so important because that is what you are here for – to figure out how to move the organization forward." Negative thought patterns are repetitive and unproductive. They serve no real purpose and cause negative emotions which are a reflection of our thoughts. Once we learn to recognize and identify these thought patterns as they occur, we have a choice about how to react. Negative thinking can take the form of expecting that bad things will happen – or that nothing good will ever happen.

When the mind casts itself into the future and conjures up scenes and thoughts about what could go wrong – or creates 'what if' scenarios, we become trapped in negative thought patterns. That leads to constantly criticizing ourselves – and others in our lives, a cause of tremendous strain on relationships.

Successful business people know the value of moving on after failure. Sony started out making rice cookers that burned the rice. Evan Williams founded Twitter after iTunes made his podcasting platform Odeo obsolete. Henry Ford's first two companies failed, leaving him broke.

Along with eBay, Priceline is one of the few dot-com era Web companies that were able to effectively stage comebacks. Though the company made waves with its bold strategy in the early 2000s of 'name your price' for airfare and hotel rooms, the revolution fizzled. Through competitor acquisitions and trimming Priceline's product offerings, CEO Jeffrey Boyd was able to return the company to profitability. He argues that he had to push a lot of internal and external negativity aside. Today, Priceline is a titan of the travel industry.

General Motors faced disaster in 2009 when it filed for bankruptcy and laid off thousands of workers. The U.S. government stepped in much against public opinion. After trimming costs and closing several divisions, it went public again, raising $20 billion. By 2013, the government had sold off the last of its GM shares: a remarkable positive turnaround that saved a million jobs. One of the most expensive price malfunctions was Alitalia Airlines' slip-up in 2006. The airline accidentally marked a business-class flight from Toronto to Cyprus at $39 instead of $3,900, and 2,000 tickets were sold at this price. Alitalia quickly agreed to honour the tickets, which amounted to a $7.72 million loss. But the brand benefits were huge and any negativity was dissipated.

Dwelling on mistakes made in the past creates negativity. Feelings of guilt and worthlessness may arise when we play over and over in our mind 'bad' choices or 'wrong' actions we think we've made. But, there's nothing negative about simply reflecting on past experiences.

The practice

- By focusing on positive thoughts, you become aware and mindful. Step back from a problem and become the observer as it's easier to think in a balanced way.

- Focus more on the 'now'.

- Try yoga or meditation.

- Don't worry about what *could* go wrong in a situation. Think instead about what could (and possibly will) go right.

14 ADDRESS PROBLEMS

Problems are barriers to mindset change. Of course, we all have problems of some sort. It's part of life. Some are easier than others to solve. Some require help and some you just can't shift. But if you step back from the problem then several things occur – the problem diminishes and you can see solutions more clearly.

The idea

In 1993, a syringe was allegedly found in a can of Diet Pepsi in Washington DC. The following week, more than fifty reports of Diet Pepsi can-tampering were reported. Both PepsiCo and the FDA were confident that the reports were false, so Pepsi defended itself against the accusations. But Pepsi didn't make vague 'trust me' statements; four videos were produced each pinpointing the manufacturing process and safety. Diet Pepsi sales had fallen 2 per cent during the crisis, but recovered within a month.

In 2010, Toyota recalled over 8 million vehicles for safety defects, including a problem where the car's accelerator jammed, which had caused multiple deaths. Toyota initially couldn't work out the problem, but it sent out PR teams to stop the media backlash anyway. To begin with, management was invisible. Toyota's response was slow, with devastating results. But it was a wake-up call for the company – and the result was a mix of extended warranties, increased marketing, leveraging its long-term track record and reassuring consumers about safety. Its ads in the following months were sincere, showing the company's dedication to fixing the problem. Toyota's executives became visible.

We often have a self-centred view of the world, leading us to think only of the negative ways a problem could affect us. But if we think of the problem, any problem, as a separate entity, unrelated to us, we'll do a better job of tempering our emotions and thinking about the difficulty objectively. One helpful strategy to do this is to describe the problem as if it were happening to someone else.

Rather than seeing problems as heavy forces of opposition, successful people see problems as opportunities (mostly). Chris-Craft began building wooden boats in 1881. Between the 1950s to the late 1960s, the business had 80 per cent of the yacht manufacturing market. Then fiberglass yachts took market share. In less than ten years, Chris-Craft went from being the dominant yacht builder to bankruptcy. Chris-Craft sales people said that fiberglass was just a fad. Management refused to admit that the era of wooden luxury yachts was over. They couldn't see the changing business climate or future opportunities. They didn't address the problem.

Seeing a problem as an opportunity reduces the stress that usually accompanies any new problem – because the problem is viewed in an irritating light first and then a positive one. A growth mindset will always support positivity.

The practice

- Look at a problem as if it wasn't yours. What would you say to the problem's owner?

- Accept the problem. It exists. That doesn't mean you have to give in to it or be violent in response. You can also stop putting more energy into the problem and feeding it. Address it.

- Ask yourself: 'what's the worst that can happen?' You can easily blow problems all out of proportion. So, don't.

- Let go of the need to be right. Open your mind to a solution that may work and try it out instead of just making snap judgements based on little information. .

15 DON'T STRESS

STRESS CAN HARM YOU – and worse. Also, the pressure of whatever is stressing you will stop you from growth. Your head will be full of stuff that allows for no clarity and no opportunity to change.

The idea

Microsoft co-founder Bill Gates apparently likes to read before bed. He reads for at least an hour, no matter how late it is. It's relaxing, he says. Gates has also said that something he learned from Warren Buffett was to keep things simple. That too creates less stress. Gates comments that Buffet has the "ability to boil things down, to just work on the things that really count, to think through the basics; it's so amazing that he can do that. It's a special form of genius." In other words, strip away all the fuss and it's easier to focus on a task. And by the way, Warren Buffet, plays the ukulele to relax.

After receiving an honorary degree from The University of Glasgow, Apple CEO Tim Cook advised students to stay positive and disregard much of the 'noise' that surrounds us. Listening to everyone all the time is incredibly stressful. "In today's environment, the world is full of cynics and you have to tune them out," he said. "Because if not, they become a cancer in your mind, in your thinking and you begin thinking that you can't or that life is negative." For Facebook COO Sheryl Sandberg, it isn't so much about what she does, but what she doesn't do. She turns off her phone at night – no email, no calls, no Internet.

If left unchecked, stress and anxiety can have long-term negative health results. People have different tolerances for and to stress – one person's panic-inducing confrontation is another person's stimulating discussion. Whereas traditional 'fight or flight' situations were over quickly, today 'issues' drag on. As a result, we live with the harmful effects of mini shots of adrenalin and cortisol constantly hitting our blood supply. Our bodies aren't able to distinguish the origin or severity of the stress so we end up with one 'pool' of worry. If this pool gets too full before we're able to fight the stress, then inability to cope and panic follow. Fast.

Coping is an important part of problem-solving. Sometimes we have to turn the problem around, not just as an opportunity but to make life easier. At IKEA, you may have wondered about the intriguing Swedish product names. You may have thought it was a gimmick, but it's not. Ingvar Kamprad, the company's founder, worried that his dyslexia made it hard to remember product codes. So, he created a system to associate product names with a visual image. Less stress.

The practice

- It is said that looking at our laptops and phone screens late at night can prevent our bodies from releasing melatonin, which helps us sleep.

- When you're feeling overwhelmed, it's important to find out why. Feeling out of control and under pressure is a form of emotional overloading and can also trigger release of stress hormones.

- Walking can provide an immediate change of scenery and body chemistry that can reduce stress.

- Talk the matter through with someone (maybe on a walk) who will a) listen properly and b) tell you the truth.

- The ability to say no is important provided you have a reason for saying no.

16 DON'T TAKE YOURSELF TOO SERIOUSLY

TAKING OURSELVES TOO SERIOUSLY can become a barrier to change because we don't see the ordinary side of life – some of which is funny and fun – and the funny and fun are helpful to positive thinking. Balance and calm are key ingredients for happiness. As is smiling.

The idea

Recounting his involvement in a media stunt that Virgin did in 1999, where the firm flew a blimp with the tagline 'BA can't get it up' over the not-yet-complete London Eye, Richard Branson said: "Being a bit cheeky and having a bit of fun is good – not taking yourself too seriously is important." Sometimes it can be hard to laugh at yourself and not take life so seriously. There's the demands of family, relationships and work that often make it hard to look for levity. And, of course, we all do have an ego and it's easy to feel crushed if our ego is hurt. Nobody likes being made a fool of in front of other people. If we're able to laugh at ourselves though, we can make ourselves and others feel better. Obviously, if someone is being highly offensive or rude, then that's not funny and needs managing.

When we take ourselves less seriously, we're able to see the humour in situations. There are clearly times in life that are genuinely serious. However, far too often we add unnecessary stress, pressure and negativity to situations with an inability to see the funny side. The Bell Leadership Institute's founder, Dr. Gerald D. Bell, wrote, "Humor is a vital tool of leadership. People… are often surprised that 'sense of humor' is the phrase most frequently associated with the best in leaders. Those who can combine a strong work ethic and sense of humor may have the leading edge in their organizations."

A smile counts a lot for all of us both as givers and receivers. Marketers (sometimes) use humour to great effect. Old Spice is an example. Look at their Twitter page and their ads. Their marketing works because, even though their products are for men, women are entertained and drawn in too. Lighten up about yourself too. We all have quirks. Consider the things that people like about you and the things that they may like less. Laugh or, at least smile, at the things that you do or say that might make people laugh with (not at) you. Laughter relieves stress and boredom, boosts engagement and well-being – and spurs not only creativity and collaboration but also productivity. Laughter helps shift our perspective and it also has a positive impact on our physiology – relaxing muscles, boosting the immune systems, releasing endorphins, decreasing stress hormones and increasing blood flow.

Laughter and smiling are usually contagious and make for a comfortable atmosphere and ensure that teamwork (and you) work better.

The practice

- A priest, a rabbi, an imam and a nun walk into a bar and the bartender says, 'What is this, a joke?'"

- If you can't be 'ha-ha' funny, at least be 'aha!' funny. Cleverness is sometimes good enough.

- Realise that some people may not like you and that's okay. It's life.

17 DON'T BE A VICTIM

President Lyndon Johnson's Secretary of Health, Education and Welfare, John W. Gardner, wrote, "Self-pity is easily the most destructive of the non-pharmaceutical narcotics; it is addictive, gives momentary pleasure and separates the victim from reality." Being a victim will not allow you to grow. For the most part, you create *your* future – so take responsibility.

The idea

Societies (and the media) are quick to assign blame as to why something did or didn't happen. People too readily point accusingly at other people. The responses are along the lines of 'it's not fair' and 'if only' and 'it's not my fault'. We relinquish all power when we say or think these things. We have to decide that it's up to us to manage ourselves and not pass blame to someone else. Sometimes that's not possible but mostly it is. We should shout a big 'stop' when we become defensive and ready to blame anyone or anything else.

In 1954, Elvis Prestley performed for the first time at the Grand Ole Opry in Tennessee. Jimmy Denny, the venue's manager, fired Elvis after just one performance and apparently said to him, "You ain't goin' nowhere, son. You ought to go back to drivin' a truck." Presley refused to be a victim.

We all get caught in the victim-trap from time to time – feeling as if we've been wronged. Feeling like a victim only makes us feel worse. If we wallow in victim status, it's maybe because we think that it will get us what we want (care, concern, love, the job, the promotion.) That's how we thought as a child. We may think that being a victim will make us feel better. The main reason feeling like a victim leads to unhappiness is because it means we identify with being powerless. And powerlessness equals fear and fear equals unhappiness. It's nigh on impossible to be powerless and happy at the same time.

When we feel sorry for ourselves, the world seems to be against us. But not everyone. Sara Blakely, the founder of Spanx, refused to give up on her invention, despite people telling her that her idea was ridiculous. When approaching lawyers about her concept of formfitting, footless pantyhose, several thought the idea a joke. She was treated with similar disdain by hosiery manufacturers. Finally, a mill owner returned Blakely's calls. While he thought the idea was crazy, his two daughters thought differently. Blakely went on to turn her initial $5,000 investment into $1 billion.

Bad things happen to everyone from time to time. Pitying yourself and wanting others to feel sorry for you isn't going to make things better. Victims often hold on to feelings of bitterness and anger from past hurts. That colours their experiences in the present and helps nobody.

The practice

- When you feel like a victim, what you're forgetting is this: no one else is responsible for your experience in life. Of course, you *are* affected by what other people say and do, but ultimately your sense of well-being is dependent on you.

- Blaming others may provide temporary relief from your pain but, in the long run, it will solve nothing – unless it's a law suit and even then, it may solve nothing of course.

- Stop blaming yourself for everything that goes wrong. Things go wrong – that's life – but they also go right.

- A victim is jealous of someone else's success – a survivor is inspired by it.

18 DON'T BLAME YOUR PARENTS

THIS IS SOMETHING THAT's easy to do – because it's a natural port of call in the blame stakes. But, unless something horrendous happened to you as a child, you need to take responsibility as an adult for everything that you think, believe and do.

The idea

As children, we see our parents as infallible. There's a deep sense of security that comes with knowing that our parents always have the answer, always know what's right and always know what to do next. But at some point, we realise that our parents are flawed. Just like everyone.

Maye Musk, the mother of Elon Musk, founder of SpaceX and Tesla, was the sole breadwinner for her three sons after her divorce from their father and did everything to improve the futures of her children. Elon admires his mother's work ethic as a force behind his success. She had several jobs and accepted another at the University of Toronto so that he could get a free education. And tennis champion Andy Murray's dedication to perfection is undoubtedly down to his mother Judy's determination.

After Indrani Nooyi became Pepsi's CEO, people began complimenting her mother on how she raised her. That made Nooyi realise the large role parents played in the success of their children. As a result, she began writing personal letters to hundreds of employees' parents to express her gratitude.

But, conversely, many people go through a phase where they blame their parents for the negative aspects of who, what and where they are.

That's good in one sense – it's useful to reflect on the past to get insight into the present. Of course, there are those who were terribly treated as children and the negativity that followed is understandable. However, generally speaking, there is no value in blaming our upbringing for any negative aspects of our lives. We are inevitably in part a product of our parents and upbringing: behaviours, attitudes, awareness, education. However, we're *not* an exact replica and we can have different beliefs. Not easy of course sometimes. We do have a choice to be different from our parents. We must not feel trapped in a direction that's dictated by someone else's choices, bias and judgements. We may see things differently from our parents and that doesn't imply that their ways of thinking were wrong. Just different. And also, importantly, society and culture now will have changed from 'then': politics, work, money, relationships, attitudes, technology.

To hold our parents responsible for any negative influence on our lives is to return to the mindset of a child – a mindset where we feel entitled to have everything fixed for us and where we perceive the responsibility for our lives to be outside of ourselves. This position is understandable, but it's something that we must let go.

The practice

- Your parents determine some aspects of what you are, but they don't necessarily have to determine everything or indeed anything. You are you.

- No matter how much you think your parents deserve your vitriol and resentment, these things serve no positive purpose and the process may hurt you more than them.

- You are responsible for the majority of your current 'you'.

- The only thing you can change about the past, is how you let it affect you now.

19 GET YOUR BODY LANGUAGE TALKING

How WE STAND, SIT and hold ourselves – in any situation – describes a picture for any observer. It affects you and anyone with whom you engage. It affects how people think of you and how you feel about you.

The idea

In a 2003 University of Colgate study, neuroscientists studying the effects of hand gestures and speech, found that when a speaker's gestures didn't match what was being said – the listeners switched off. It's the same dip that occurs when people listen to anything that doesn't make immediate sense. If a message is inconsistent, we stop trying to make sense of it. Also, if someone uses pleasant and happy words but with negative body language, then our brains are wired to default and negative judgment. Similarly, voice makes a difference. We hear Ian McKellen as Gandalf and we like the tone and the comfort his voice brings.

James and Rupert Murdoch testified a few years ago for a Parliamentary inquiry board into the UK's *News of the World* phone hacking controversy. These are powerful media moguls under fire for a scandal with criminal and ethical implications. The father-son team was unified and shared the same message. But what came across was very different. News Corp Chairman Rupert Murdoch was solid, confident, strong. He looked his accusers in the eye during questioning. He leaned in towards the panel and used only a few deliberate gestures to make his point. Even though he couldn't remember details, he never wavered. His son's body language though was jittery and nervous. He fidgeted, shifted his shoulders and his repeated use of the same hand gestures was distracting.

Mark Zuckerberg apparently imitates others' body language while having a conversation demonstrating that one is in agreement with the other person. Also, though it sounds strange, it can help us to understand what someone else is thinking. We might not yet have achieved the fame and fortune that Elon Musk has, but that shouldn't stop us from power posing as he does with a confident smile and stance in front of, say, a new Tesla. Social psychologist, Amy Cuddy, said during a TED Talk that, "it's possible that when you pretend to be powerful, you're more likely to actually feel powerful." The alignment between body and mind is so strong that our body language directly affects our mood and mindset. And vice versa. How we act in front of people each time is important. It tells a story. But, it mustn't tell an arrogant one.

Imagine yourself feeling happy, energetic and on top of the world. What do you picture? You probably have a little more bounce in your step. You're smiling, your chin is high and your body feels relaxed. When we see an old friend, we smile. Everything we do is open. We can picture it because this is how we all look and act when we feel great. When we feel low, we move more sluggishly. We're closed off and spend more time looking down.

Most people have no idea that the majority of our communication is non-verbal. In other words, it's not just *what* we say, it's *how* we say it too. If we go into a pitch, interview or date and only focus on the words we use, we're leaving our most powerful tool behind. Jack Ma is fond of the double thumbs-up. In China, this gesture can be seen as a reference to Buddha. The gesture translates as similarly positive elsewhere. He's had setbacks. He failed his college entrance exam twice and his first business, *China Yellow Pages*, was a failure. He's also said that he was rejected by Harvard many times. So, he's successful now and is trying to unconsciously encourage others. The thumbs-up is Ma's way of saying: 'Don't give up!'

The practice

- Putting on a smiling face (and meaning it) can actually trigger feelings of happiness in others – and in you. The firing of facial muscles when you smile is linked to the experience of happiness.

- The perfect handshake is brief, firm but not tight and uses the whole hand, not just the fingertips. It conveys confidence and positivity.

- If you want people to focus on you in a meeting or during a conversation, speak up, look at them and don't multi-task. Avoid the temptation to check your text messages, your watch or how the other participants are reacting. Instead, focus on those to whom you are speaking. And listen. *Show* you're listening.

- Stand and sit up straight.

- Be authentic.

JARGON: DON'T USE IT

WE'RE SURROUNDED BY PHRASES that mean only something to the speaker and his/her colleagues. If we don't understand, we say nothing or are marginalized. That's a negative and cannot help your growth mindset prosper. Speaking and using plain, direct language can.

The idea

It's said that the American navy described an aircraft crash as 'a semi-controlled descent into local indigenous terrain.' A 2011 study conducted by New York University concluded that abstract language leads listeners to believe a speaker is lying more than when plain language is used. This comes as no surprise; abstract language evades facts and is sometimes intended to confuse. It gives the speaker gravitas. But it's a false gravitas. That's not to say that all jargon-users are liars; some are just trying to fit in with their contemporaries. But the use of vapid expressions is often an attempt to convey a point without considering whether or not the correct point is being conveyed, or whether or not the point is worth conveying at all. Life is full of jargon – and trying to understand all of it is hard and often leads to poor communication and mistakes.

Jack Weiss, president of Coco Pazzo restaurants, Chicago, says he hears – and uses – jargon frequently 'on the floor.' Waiters who don't show up are MIA – missing in action. Volatile individuals are 'toxic'. Wine that tastes phenomenal is 'nectar'. An extreme restaurant emergency – such as an unprepared kitchen during a rush, or even a kitchen fire – is a 'meltdown'. Clientele who hold highly regarded positions are 'literati'. Weiss says those terms improve team communication. And that's fine *if* everyone understands. Jomaree Pinkard, co-founder of

Hella Cocktail Co., a U.S. business that produces non-alcoholic mixers for cocktails, admits jargon makes him cringe, but he still uses it daily, because it's easy. When asked to name a favourite jargon term, he replied, "We hate them all equally, but if we had to choose... it would be 'punt' (to delay solving a problem or implementing a feature until later). But... it'll fall into the 'most ridiculous' bucket shortly."

Not that long ago, on the BBC World Service there was a 39-word jargon-ridden answer provided by the Starbucks' CEO to the question: "Will you buy any more companies this year?" The proper answer should have been: "No."

In 2013, Frits van Paasschen, then CEO of Starwood Hotels & Resorts Worldwide, said in an interview, "One thing that has struck me over time is the importance of being able to speak and communicate clearly. There's no need to dress up your strategy or your goals in elaborate prose. Plain, simple, declarative sentences about what we're trying to do, what we need to do and the way we do business, is an important part of leading... I would say I have an aversion to jargon... I hate jargon..."

Some might say that there's an internal pride in having our own language short cuts. People think that they know something that outsiders don't and it's nice to feel like we're part of a group of people which uses the same terms. But jargon can waste time and money when documents, emails and instructions take longer to read or understand. Time is wasted when unknown terms have to be explained or are interpreted incorrectly. If a nurse can't understand what is being asked of her/him, what are the chances of it being done properly or at all?

Bart Engal, CEO of The Humphrey Group, maintains that, "What I concluded was that though there are some benefits to jargon, these benefits are almost always outweighed by negatives. The result: if you want to influence and persuade others when you communicate, you are almost always better off replacing jargon with clear, powerful language... Some audiences simply shut down when they hear too many words they don't understand, tuning out the speaker completely... Leaders know every word they use should support their message – or be discarded. Leaders should focus on defining and sharing powerful ideas with their audiences. They know that the words they select should convey – rather than cloud – their thinking."

It's never a sign of cleverness to use empty phrases, not to mention mixed metaphors. People tend to fall back on corporate or social buzzwords when they feel a need to demonstrate that they're in control. Of course, we do that most often when we *don't* feel in control and jargon ends up communicating the opposite: ironically enough, its hallmark is the lack of resolution that vocabulary conveys, not its clarity.

The practice

- Stop using words that aren't in the dictionary.

- Use words that your audience will understand.

- The way we talk and write affects the way people see us.

- Some people feel that using jargon makes them sound clever. Wrong. If anything, it can make them look stupid. On the other hand, if your industry relies on shorthand speech and it saves time – and if everyone understands – that's fine, but only within that group.

- You'll be a breath of fresh air if you master the art of simple communication.

- In business, when people don't understand what you're saying, you could be missing out on a great deal. Literally.

CHAPTER 3
MINDSET CHANGE IS ALL ABOUT HELPING YOURSELF

SIMPLIFY

LOTS OF CLUTTER – in any sense – makes it hard to focus on mindset change. You concentrate on the wrong things and you tend to have too many things on which to focus. From IKEA to Dyson to Apple to Airbnb, there's one thing that 21st century business success stories all have in common. They simplify. Simplification equals clarity and clarity equals ease of process and enjoyment.

The idea

Actor Bruce Lee said, "Hack away at the unessential." The busier and more complicated our lives, the harder it is to remain positive. When we have too many demands and obligations, with little time for fun, reflection, relationships or exercise, the more stressed we're likely to feel. Nothing ever gets properly completed and our 'to do' list gets no shorter.

Our lives can get hectic and overwhelming. Simplifying our lives helps us combat these feelings. However, living a simpler life in what can be a complex world takes some doing. Learning to create a more balanced space in our lives can help – and taking little steps is the best way to make that happen. Eliminating clutter, getting organized, simplifying relationships and learning to take time to slow down can help to keep us focused on changing our mindset.

We can't always be in constant motion and still be at our best. Ironically slowing down can also mean we get more (not less) done. Steve Jobs wrote, "That's been one of my mantras – focus and simplicity. Simple can be harder than complex – you have to work hard to get your thinking clean to make it simple. But it's worth it in the end because once you get there, you can move mountains."

We are of course spending more of our time obsessively checking texts, blogs, tweets. Walk down a street, any city street, anywhere in the world and there you have it. As fantastic as technology is, we need to make regular time to disconnect and simplify. Wrote Richard Branson, "Complexity is your enemy. Any fool can make something complicated. It is hard to make something simple."

Ryanair simplifies on price. By offering rock bottom priced flights, the airline was able to multiply the size of its market and establish itself as the UK's leading budget carrier. Similarly, Apple always simplifies its product lines. While some electronics' companies flood the market with choice, Apple chooses to perfect a handful of devices. This gives it a sense of exclusivity even though the products aren't exclusive. The same can even be said for McDonald's and its success turning the humble Big Mac into a worldwide icon. When McDonald's was first set up in 1948, the classic American coffee shop menu which traditionally had hundreds of items on it was reduced to nine.

The practice

- If we don't need something, or if it doesn't serve a positive purpose, dispose of it. Throw away or sell things you never use.

- Schedule a few days to streamline your life.

- Limit your options. There is a power in limiting choices.

- Forget multi-tasking and instead focus simply on one thing at a time until completion and then move onto the next task.

- Learn to say a polite 'No, thank you' to invitations that don't fit in with what you want to do. Learn to protect space in your diary.

- Everything being a priority actually means nothing is a priority.

NEVER EVER STOP LEARNING

"IF YOU THINK YOU know everything, how smart can you be?" somebody tweeted. A growth mindset necessitates learning. Learning is implicit to anything involving growth. Learning anything valid is positive.

The idea

Learning can be frustrating. But it doesn't need to be dull and neither should it be. At a time when the idea of business blogging was brand new (and usually feared), IBM encouraged its 320,000 employees to start company blogs. Management created a corporate blogging policy and training programme that encouraged employees to be themselves, speak in the first person and respect their co-workers. The result was a marketing bonanza. Their blogs are some of the most trusted technology writings and generate vast numbers of page-views and links back to IBM.

We worry about the time we need for learning, but these days it's easier. Ted Talks are good examples. We can learn much about subjects in which we thought we'd have no interest. There are always new skills to take on board, techniques to adopt and a host of qualifications to follow. The most successful people in any walk of life don't behave as if they know everything. They understand the fact that they have to continuously learn to be successful.

Corporate life should recognize the benefit of learning – and sharing that learning. However, employees disengage because they feel unsupported in learning, over-scrutinized or that their very jobs are at risk. And when employees feel unsafe, they're in a high-stress state where they can't concentrate and look for distractions. Companies that invest in quality employee learning succeed more. Facebook, Apple, Hyatt, Mars, Google – invest heavily in their own employees for good ideas. Realizing the power of teaching, they promote from within and support their staff to learn new skills for self-benefit and benefit to the company.

Pixar President, Ed Catmull, says, "Pixar University helps reinforce the mindset that we're all learning and it's fun to learn together." The Container Store, specializing in storage and organizing solutions, has an employee-first culture. Chairman Kip Tindell saw employee satisfaction as the key to customer satisfaction, reasoning that if a company took care of its employees, they would in turn take care of customers. To put this philosophy into practice, Tindell prioritized paying and training his employees better than the competition. His hiring philosophy revolves around first hiring great people and then giving them great training. He felt that one great employee equals three good employees. To transform new hires into great employees, The Container Store offers over 263 hours of formal training to employees during their first year, which contrasts with the industry average of 8 hours.

Starbucks gives new employees 70 per cent of their training through on-the-job experience and hands-on practice, 20 per cent through mentorship and feedback from peers, managers and learning coaches and 10 per cent from an online curriculum. Starbucks has also integrated its on-the-job training with a formal academic programme at Starbucks University through which employees also receive tuition reimbursement benefits. Putting its commitment to employee training into practice, Starbucks once closed all of its U.S. stores for three hours in 2008 in order to let employees focus on learning how to better serve coffee. That cost millions of dollars in lost revenue but CEO Howard Schultz saw the lost income as an investment.

The practice

- Building on your strengths is easier that overcoming your weaknesses. If you have a glaring gap in your skills, maybe address it now. Ben Franklin said, "An investment in knowledge pays the best interest."

- A growth mindset shows that we are responsible for our own learning and growth. When that appetite is matched by an organization's support, the result is hugely positive and beneficial.

- In today's speedy world, if we don't keep learning, we're not necessarily standing still, but we could be falling behind.

- Admit what you don't know – that's a first step to learning what you may *need* to know.

TAKE YOUR TIME BECAUSE IT'S USUALLY YOURS TO TAKE

Even if we're in the worst of moods, taking the time to look at all the beautiful and fascinating things that surround us in the world can provide an instant way to lift spirits.

The idea

'Nature-deficit disorder' is a phrase used by Richard Louv in his book, *Last Child in the Woods: Saving Our Children From Nature-Deficit Disorder*. He feels that our indoor lifestyles are contributing to a wide range of health and behavioural problems. Positive people connect with nature and the outdoors. Duke Senior in Shakespeare's *As You Like It* says in Act II, scene 1, "And this our life, exempt from public haunt, finds tongues in trees, books in the running brooks, sermons in stones, and good in everything. I would not change it." When we were children, everything was new and therefore a source of wonder. We rapidly become accustomed to our surroundings. And yet, watching a large aircraft land or take off is still astonishing to many people as is a huge ship moving majestically up the Bosphorous or watching a car being built by robots or an ant carrying a hundred times its own weight or the trees in autumn. Size, nature and scientific wonder are awe-inspiring still.

When we work hard, it's nice to have an employer that lets us play hard, too. Some big-name companies, such as Glassdoor and Virgin Group, offer unlimited time off. However, this type of policy usually discourages employees from actually taking vacation days because there's no incentive to 'use it or lose it.' Many companies urge employees to take days to just walk and discover new things. Facebook offers some incredible perks for parents and parents-to-be: new mothers or fathers get four months of paid parental leave, reimbursement for day care and adoption fees and several thousand dollars after their child is born. Similarly, US fast-food restaurant chain Capriotti's Sandwich Shop allows its staff to take time off, no questions asked, to attend their children's events and activities.

For every five years employees have been at Epic Systems, they are eligible for a four-week paid sabbatical. In addition, if they choose to travel during this time, the company helps fund the trip for each employee and one guest. Similarly, Fizziology, a social media research firm, offers travel stipends to employees. They call it 'For Your Inspiration Trips', which are encouraged for each worker every year.

We should be able to appreciate the immense beauty that we usually take for granted. It just takes a bit of concentration and mindfulness. For example, think about how many different processes have to be organized simply to create the experience you're having right now. Imagine if all of that was a conscious effort. Imagine if you had to think about breathing or about listening to music. Every breath, every movement and every condition that's creating the possibility for us to be alive right now is extraordinary. We often get inundated with our lists or get caught up in the drama of things that aren't really important. Most of the time we only catch a glimpse of how amazing things really are before we get sucked back into the monotony of our routines. We lose mindfulness.

Beauty is not always realised through a life-changing moment or a great epiphany. It's not always hidden in a rainbow, in an earth-shattering orgasm or in skydiving at 15,000 feet. Beauty is often looking into a person's eyes, in a flower, in paint peeling off an old fence or in the clever design of an everyday object. It's often where you least expect it.

The practice

- There are 168 hours in every week. You probably spend 40 at work, leaving you with 128 to sleep, eat, rest, and spend however you want.

- Without calm and order, your mindset won't alter. Neither will it develop unless you take time out to appreciate what's around you.

- Find beauty in the little things. If your mind is brooding or if you're distracted, you'll miss them.

- Allow yourself to view things again as if for the first time.

- Allow yourself time to enjoy relationships and your family.

- Don't count your misfortunes and all the things that are lacking *before* you count your blessings and all that you already have.

READ AND READ SOME MORE

READING IS FUN, USEFUL, educational and relaxing. Anything that creates added value to change and growth will benefit you. Storytelling is one of these stimuli.

The idea

Storytelling plays a big part in mindset development. If we listen to someone giving a PowerPoint presentation with boring bullet points, only certain parts of the brain get activated. Scientists call these Broca's and Wernicke's areas. Overall, we decode words into meaning. And that's it, nothing else happens. There's no trigger, no excitement. When we are being told a story, though, things change dramatically. If the story's told well (films, plays, operas, books) then the language (or music, acting, characters) activates our brain with all guns firing.

Warren Buffet reads a lot. "I read 500 pages every day. That's how knowledge works. It builds up, like compound interest. All of you can do it, but I guarantee not many of you will do it." He still devotes about 80 per cent of each day to reading. And he's not alone. Bill Gates reads about 50 books per year. Mark Cuban reads more than three hours every day. Elon Musk is an avid reader and, when asked how he learned to build rockets, he said, "I read books." Successful people are highly selective about what they read, opting to be educated over being entertained. They believe that books are a gateway to learning and knowledge. According to Tom Corley, author of *Rich Habits: The Daily Success Habits of Wealthy Individuals*, rich people read for self-improvement, education and success. Whereas others read primarily to be entertained. Business leaders in particular like biographies and autobiographies of other successful people for guidance and inspiration.

Elon Musk likes the biographies of great inventors and entrepreneurs, like Howard Hughes, Benjamin Franklin, Albert Einstein and, of course, Nikola Tesla: "Franklin's autobiography is the most influential book in my own life... I love stories of all kinds, but nothing motivates me more than real-life tales of ambitious people." Bill Gates likes *Tap Dancing to Work: Warren Buffett on Practically Everything, 1966-2012* by Carol Loomis. He also likes *The Sixth Extinction: An Unnatural History* by Elizabeth Kolbert. Barack Obama likes *Song of Solomon* by Toni Morrison, *Moby-Dick, Parting the Waters: America in the King Years* by Taylor Branch, *Gilead* by Marilynne Robinson and *Self-Reliance* by Ralph Waldo Emerson. He also enjoys reading the Bible, Shakespeare's tragedies and Lincoln's collected writings.

Stories are helpful. A story can put our whole brain to work. A story can be in various forms and can apply to fiction, instruction, research and non-fiction. A story, if broken down into the simplest form, is a connection of cause and effect. And that's exactly how we think. We think in narratives all day long, no matter if what we're thinking about is solving a problem, dinner tomorrow evening, our partner, our children, a movie or our careers. Or whatever.

This isn't surprising since stories make up 65 per cent of our conversations. That's why metaphors work so well. Whilst we imagine, we activate a part of our brains called the insula which helps us relate to that same experience as that which is being told or that which we're reading about. That applies to pain, emotion, joy, anger, warmth, hate, love, excitement and sex. Interestingly, overused and banal language elicits zero response or low memorability – so *how* we tell stories has to be done well.

With reading we're guided by a writer who sucks us into other worlds and new ideas. Reading helps us to develop our own ideas, language and personalities. Reading can increase our emotional intelligence. It stimulates positivity and is enormously satisfying.

The practice

- Reading helps prevent stress, avoid depression and dementia, and enhances confidence, empathy and decision-making.

- Read great books, great blogs, great articles. That's a very subjective comment – but you will know what you like, what's positive, interesting and informative. Be selective. Choose the best. Develop a sense of what stretches you as well as what helps your (maybe new) beliefs.

- The more you read, the more you learn.

- When you read a book, you have to remember an assortment of characters, backgrounds, ambitions, history and nuances, as well as facts and sub-plots that weave their way through every story. Every new memory you create forges new synapses (brain pathways) and strengthens existing ones, which assists in short-term memory recall.

- When you're reading fiction or biographies, your ability to empathize is improved. Putting yourself in someone else's shoes undeniably helps your mindset growth and attitude (predominantly one and the same thing of course).

GET SOME SLEEP

Sleep refreshes and is energizing. And you need energy to be positive, to learn and to grow.

The idea

For leaders like Apple CEO Tim Cook, who apparently awakes at 3:45 every morning to begin work on the 700-emails he receives each day, sleep gets in the way of staying on top of their responsibilities. Is that a good thing? Chrysler Fiat CEO Sergio Marchionne wakes up at 3:30am to check European markets. PepsiCo CEO Indra Nooyi studied at Yale while moonlighting as a receptionist from midnight to 5am. Marissa Mayer, CEO of Yahoo!, was known to sleep four hours a night so that she could allegedly do a 130-hour work week. However, in 2014, she allegedly missed an important dinner with chief executives due to an overdue nap, after being awake for 20 hours. It's a good reminder that unnatural behaviour has its consequences.

Sleeping less than eight hours each night didn't quite work for *Huffington Post* founder Arianna Huffington, who collapsed from sleep deprivation due to 18-hour work days. Since then, she's become a champion of proper sleep.

Most people don't get enough sleep and some think that shows guts and grit. Rubbish. If we're tired all the time, we can't achieve. When we have more energy throughout the day, we achieve more of what we want to do. Think of sleep as a most precious resource. Too little of it and we lose focus and its loss has the potential to damage personal and professional relationships.

Lack of sleep has been linked to higher rates of depression and the accompanying spirals. Its lack causes exhaustion and wears down mental faculties. A regular sleeping cycle promotes our general physical health. OK, a very few people (around 5 per cent of the world's population) can manage on little sleep, but many of those will take daily naps (e.g. John F Kennedy and Winston Churchill). A strong proponent of the eight-hour circadian rhythm, Jeff Bezos avoids morning meetings to eat a healthy breakfast with his wife and children. Bill Gates emphasises the importance of at least seven hours of sleep to be creative.

The practice

- Sleep allows you to better do what you need to do when you're awake. Obvious? One would have thought so.

- Getting in sync with your body's natural sleep-wake cycle, or circadian rhythm, is one of the most important strategies for sleeping better.

- Avoid sleeping in – even on weekends. If you need to make up for a late night, opt for a daytime nap.

- If you get sleepy way before your bedtime, get off the couch and do something which necessitates standing up.

- Melatonin is a naturally occurring hormone controlled by light exposure that helps regulate your sleep-wake cycle. Your brain secretes more melatonin when it's dark – making you sleepy – and less when it's light – making you more alert. However, many aspects of modern life can alter your body's production of melatonin and shift your circadian rhythm.

- Avoid late-night television, messaging or emails – too stimulating.

- People who exercise regularly sleep better.

- If you wake during the night feeling anxious about something, make a brief note of it on paper and postpone worrying about it until the next day when it will be easier to resolve.

26 DOODLE

Doodling aids cognitive performance and recollection. You need both for mindset development.

The idea

After Somali militiamen killed eighteen U.S. soldiers in October 1993, President Clinton convened his national-security team. He sat silently while being briefed. Then, his aide Richard Clarke recalled, "When they had talked themselves out, Clinton stopped doodling and looked up. 'Okay, here's what we're going to do.'"

Dwight Eisenhower drew images of tables, pencils and himself with a head full of hair. Ronald Reagan gave cheery cartoons to staff, mostly of cowboys. John F. Kennedy reportedly doodled the word 'poverty' at the last cabinet meeting before his death. In another doodle with seeming modern-day relevance, he wrote '9/11' repeatedly and the word 'conspiracy' next to it. He also inverted the numbers, writing '11/9.' It turns out that was the tally of a committee vote, not a foreshadowing of the Sept. 11, 2001 attacks.

As Hilary Clinton sat listening to speeches on global security and the Middle East during a U.N. Security Council meeting, she was seen doodling on her speech. This news was shown in global media – alleged evidence of her lack of attention. But, just because she was doodling doesn't mean she wasn't listening or thinking. The reverse is likely.

Doodling keeps us from falling asleep or simply staring blankly when our brain has already turned off. The 'permission' to free-draw keeps us alert and aware, but slightly tuned down. Spontaneous drawings may also relieve worry, making it easier to focus. We like to make sense of our lives by making up stories, but sometimes there are gaps that can't be filled. Doodles can fill these gaps, possibly by finding lost memory pieces, bringing them to the 'here and now' and making the picture of our present state complete.

In 2014 Nike CEO Mark Parker carried a Moleskine notebook to every meeting. It was full of doodles. Parker has said that the doodles helped clarify the brainstorming process. Companies like Dell, Disney and Zappos.com, employ artists to teach staff to use visual language. Steve Jobs was known to go for long walks to think and he regularly used a small white board to sketch out possible solutions to problems.

Although doodles may look like scribbles, they're not quite as random as we might think. Some psychologists believe that doodles can reveal what is going on in the unconscious. In the same way that an EEG transmits brain activity to a piece of paper, your hand might also do the same.

The practice

- Doodling can help improve your cognitive performance on tasks such as memory retention, listening, creativity and emotional expression.

- Doodle whatever comes to mind – anything to keep your mind from falling into the default state and no longer paying attention to the outside world.

- You can use your doodles to clarify your ideas.

- Sometimes, instead of daydreaming, you need your brain to disengage, but to still be paying attention to stimuli.

27 JOIN A GROUP

THERE ARE BENEFITS TO being a member of a group or community. People feel more secure when they know that they have others around them who share their goals and care about their progress. Joining a group by and large makes people feel good – and positive.

The idea

Networks have always been important in getting things done – at the business and personal level. Leveraging who you know plays an important role in life. People join groups inside and outside of work for many reasons. Membership can provide us with social status or security and can result in some form of need satisfaction on the part of the individual. Feeling good is a precursor to doing more better.

Think about every community of which you're a part, from your group of friends to professional gatherings. We join people by liking what they like on a regular basis and vice versa – maybe weekly, monthly, annually. The location might be physical or an online forum. Rule for entry can be loose or specific depending on need and advantage of belonging. And, of course, we have to be careful since some groups can be set up for dangerous or extreme reasons.

Groups (and of course gangs) can have varying numbers of members, communication styles and structures. In most cases, all the members of the collective come together to serve or attain a common goal. Groups build on the strengths of their members. Port Sunlight is a village in Merseyside, UK, built in 1888 by Lever Brothers to accommodate workers in its soap factory. The name Port Sunlight came from the company's most popular brand of soap. The brothers believed in community and social/work groups. Religious groups also build businesses and develop groups and communities. For example, global businesses that started as Quaker work and social groups include Quaker Oats, Barclay's Bank, Sandy Spring Bank, John Hopkins University, Huntsman Steel, Cadbury's, Sony and Rowntree's.

When we're in a strong community, it's highly likely that we'll get ideas about and for our own growth. At LVMH, the world's largest luxury-goods company, there are brilliant, creative innovators like Marc Jacobs and Phoebe Philo. But alongside them there are a proportion of executives who monitor and assess ideas with an analytical business focus. One of the ingredients in LVMH's success is having a culture where opposite types can thrive and work cooperatively as internal communities.

Arup is perhaps the world's most creative engineering and design company. Many iconic buildings bear the mark of Arup's distinctive imprint: the Sydney Opera House, the Centre Pompidou, the Beijing Water Cube. Arup approaches its work holistically. When the firm builds a suspension bridge, for example, it looks beyond the concerns of the immediate client to the region and community that rely on the bridge. Arup then create groups with mathematicians, economists, artists, public representatives and politicians. Many of these groups are social, not just work related.

British retail firm John Lewis Group is a cooperative; every employee is a co-owner and shares in annual profits. It operates as a community. Staff are fiercely loyal. The company goes to great lengths to support employee interests and sub-communities.

Community and group culture (inside or out of the working environment) recognizes that in the age of Facebook, WikiLeaks, and Twitter, we're better off telling people the truth before someone else does. And that's a big plus in the world of mindset growth. Storytelling and two-way support are at the heart of group membership – knowing how to receive help, give help and help ourselves. Underlying self-help in a group is the basic theme: 'we're not alone.'

The practice

- Companionship is vital for us and an important function of group membership.

- Survival, security, learning, sharing and growth are part of 'community'.

- With group membership comes the opportunity for leadership roles.

- Groups have the capability to achieve more than an individual alone. And with a group or community you can build a useful network.

DON'T TRY AND BE HAPPY ALL OF THE TIME

We don't appreciate how happy we are until the moment has already passed and we can do no more than look back at how happy we were. Happy equals positive, but trying to be happy 100 per cent of the time is impossible. So don't try.

The idea

The happiest people don't necessarily have the best of everything, but have learned to make the best of whatever they do have. Nobody can be euphoric all the time – and trying to be so will drive the person and those around him/her nuts. Happiness is only truly understood when juxtaposed with its opposite, unhappiness or, better, lack of happiness. By desperately trying to be happy all the time, when something bad were to happen, we wouldn't be able to cope. There's a danger in happiness becoming a 'necessity' and companies can't insist on employees being perpetually upbeat. Whether we're talking about our ancestral Garden of Eden or the promise of future happiness in Heaven, Valhalla, Jannah or Vaikuntha, eternal happiness is the divine prize to many. Most of us possess the optimism bias, which is the tendency to think that our future will be better than our present.

Facebook, known for its perks and inclusive company culture, has, at time of writing, according to PayScale research, the highest number of happy employees in American businesses, with 97 per cent reporting high job satisfaction. Software company Salesforce.com came in second, with 90 per cent of employees, and utilities company Southern Co. took third place with 88 per cent of employees. But this doesn't mean that 'happy' companies are filled with people who are happy 100 per cent of time. Happiness is an elevated state. Before we experience happiness or unhappiness, we're in a state of neutrality. We don't feel either happy or unhappy, but content. Maybe being content is happy. Maybe we can reach contentment more regularly than happiness. But because happiness is so pleasant and is often readily available in different guises, we feel that it ought to be regular. Mindset growth won't develop if we try and chase a rainbow.

A good phrase for a growth mindset development is, "Isn't *this* great, right now?" Our past and future are not always superior to our present – and yet we persist in thinking that they are. We work very hard to reach a goal, anticipating the happiness it will bring. After a brief fix of 'yippee,' however, we quickly slide back to our baseline and start chasing the next carrot.

Dissatisfaction with the present and dreams of the future are what keep us motivated, while memories of the past reassure us that the feelings we seek are possible. 3M, with its 90,000 employees, is regarded as a happy company. The company offers wide benefits, but its management makes a point of communicating that being super happy isn't an expectation, but being super comfortable in what each person does is. Companies like Google, Supermedia, Unisys, GE Capital, Aecom would agree. And understanding that it's impossible to have happiness in all aspects of life all of the time can (or should) help us enjoy the happiness that we do have now.

The practice

- Don't feel that you can't discuss your worries and problems because you think you need to pretend everything is rosy all the time.

- We're all pressurized to be happy and we're told by the media that we're all responsible for our happiness and, in equal measure, to blame for our sadness. Ignore this. It's not helpful. Without life's sad, low points in life you'd never appreciate the positive.

- If you're comfortable being content, then happiness will only be a plus and the lack of happiness will only drop you back down to being content, rather than all the way down to being unhappy.

THINK 'YES. WE. CAN.'

WE TALKED ABOUT AVOIDING 'can't', but you also have to think 'can'. This was Barack Obama's proposition (and the way he said it) when he was up for re-election. Being positive opens up possibilities. But you have to believe.

The idea

"¡Si se puede!" Many people may not realise that the origin of Obama's 2008 campaign slogan was a translation of the rallying cry of the American/Mexican farm workers movement led by César E. Chávez, founder of the United Farm Workers. Wise leaders push their teams to find the possibilities of the one reason something can be achieved rather than reasons why it can't. 'Not yet' is powerful because it's much better than 'can't'. It's about knowing that with determination, perseverance and practice, we can turn 'can't' into 'can'.

We must use the word 'yet' and, for example, see our mindset growth as an unfinished process and not a pass or fail grade. Someone struggling to lose weight could say: "I haven't made my goal weight *yet* but I've already lost 10 pounds." 'Yet' means effort, a journey and growth. A growth mindset is not about being *the* best because that may mean little, but it's about you being your best. And that, in turn, is also about belief in constant step-by-step improvements under the banner of 'yes, I can'. It changes people's whole perception of what they need to do in order to be able to do it. Maybe not straight away, but in time.

The practice

- 'Yes. We. Can' blocks the naysayers. It builds positive expectations. It forges a confident team – and a confident you.

- Whenever you say you can do something, you're reinforcing that message in your mind.

- If there's something in your life which you'd like to do, but which you think you're unable to do, what's the part that you think is hard and what's the real reason behind thinking it?

- It's fine to not want to do something. But it's important to acknowledge that, if you wanted to, you could. But, if that's the case, why don't you do it?

30 TALK TO YOURSELF

Talking out loud to yourself can instil a confidence that will help you with focus and determination. It's like having a coach, but the coach is a part of you.

The idea

In 2014, the University of Michigan's Ethan Kross released a paper insisting that talking to ourselves can make us feel better about ourselves – and can help us manage challenges. It can help us motivate ourselves to achieve, he wrote. Why? Because we can debate both sides of an issue. Saying our options out loud and elaborating on the pros and cons can help bring the right choice to light and we might be surprised at the unexpected direction our thoughts take when they're audible.

Self-talking introduces optimistic thoughts – that save us from negative ones. Andre Agassi, the tennis star, wrote, "You talk to yourself and you answer yourself and you tell me if you've ever seen another sport where an athlete talks to themselves as much as they do in tennis." Talking to ourselves may seem strange because we tend to associate speaking out loud to nobody in particular as a sign of mental illness. But it's not an irrational thing to do.

Saying a name, a word or phrase out loud is a powerful retrieval method and not only does it help us perform better, it also helps us reason logically through repetition of self-affirming comments. Some people read reports and emails out loud to get a sense of argument and sense. When we talk out loud, we obviously stimulate more sensory channels than when we don't. Talking through thoughts helps us prioritize the big things affecting us.

The practice

- Using the pronoun 'you' to yourself – as in, "You're going to deliver a fantastic presentation today" – is more effective than using 'I'.

- Say, 'You can do this.'

- If you talk out loud and elaborate on the pros and cons of something, that can help bring about the right choice.

- Since talking to yourself allows you to organize your thoughts, your mind isn't constantly racing or wondering when you're going to have enough time to get it all done.

- Talking to yourself helps you prepare for difficult times in life, such as a conversation with a loved one, colleague or boss.

- Speaking to yourself helps you come up with good ideas. (So does singing in the car!)

- Verbalizing a personal plan of action may seem awkward at first ("You're going to fit into this parking space!"), but stating intentions will help you act more effectively.

CHAPTER 4
TAKING RISKS

TAKE CALCULATED RISKS

A CALCULATED RISK IS a risk that you've thought through, where you've worked out the pluses and the minuses. Successful people aren't afraid of risk, but rather they view it, not as a danger, but more of a probability that could result in positive outcomes.

The idea

Ronald Heifetz, professor at Harvard University's John F. Kennedy School of Government, said that if you make one real decision in your life, that's more than most people. Taking a real risk? Well, that's just a rarity. Bill Gates took a number of risks while co-founding Microsoft. He dropped out of college. He started his business based on a vision that the personal computer would be a useful tool in every office and home. It's said that Oracle's Larry Ellison promised customers non-existent features, only to go back to his developers and demand that they build the products with the promised features. He would also hire staff unqualified for their position only to train them later with manuals and books. Calculated risk or crazy?

While the word 'gamble' is often used interchangeably with risk, this isn't always using it in its truest sense. For FedEx CEO Fred Smith, however, the word gamble is quite appropriate. With his company struggling and in desperate need of a loan to cover fuel expenses, Smith apparently gambled the company's remaining $5,000 on a game of blackjack in Las Vegas. Was it luck, skill or intuition? Was it calculated? Whatever it was, Smith headed home from that weekend with $32,000 in his pocket.

For most of us, the benefits of risk-taking include building confidence, developing skills, having a sense of accomplishment, expressing our creativity and building emotional resilience. When we take risks, we open ourselves up to a plethora of possible outcomes – some of which may not be to our liking, even if the risk is calculated. Risk-taking can expose us to potential loss, failure, embarrassment, rejection and criticism. All of these outcomes can seem painful, but every feat that has ever been achieved required some kind of risk.

There are a wide variety of benefits that come to those who take risks; they expose themselves to new experiences, opportunities, ideas and skills. This doesn't mean that we have to take risks every day – or indeed just for the sake of it; that way lies danger. But, the moment we decide to become more of a (calculated) risk-taker is the moment we take steps that will help us break through psychological walls and overcome fears.

Robin Chase, co-founder of Zipcar and GoLoco.org, says, "In general, I am happy to take professional and entrepreneurial risks, but I'm quite risk-averse when it comes to putting my body in danger." By Chase's calculation, her decision at the age of 23 to illegally slip into Kenya from Tanzania (thus facing imprisonment or worse) was a greater risk than launching Zipcar with just $78 in her bank account.

A big barrier to risk-taking may be our need for certainty, for approval, to play it safe, to avoid feeling guilty, to rationalize – all these may be holding us back from living the life we want to live. We don't need to play it safe all the time. The habit of perfectionism will often stop us in our tracks from doing something differently and maybe, therefore, better. When we're trying to be perfect, we'll become lost in the details and the details will prevent us from taking the necessary risks that will help us to take advantage of opportunities. We have the habit of wanting guaranteed results. When it comes to risk-taking, there are no guaranteed results. It's a risk.

The practice

- Failing is both the worst and best thing that can happen to you. When you don't fail, you succeed. When you do fail, you succeed at working out another way of not doing something. If you don't risk failing, then you can't succeed.

- No outcome is ever 100 per cent certain and therefore any attempt at anything has some chance of some failure.

- Life is all about risk – you take some and you avoid others. That requires calculation and balancing what might and what might not work. An improved mindset will help you take better balanced calculations.

- Playing it safe might be habitual for you. Remember, habits are so deeply ingrained into your psyche that you often don't realise the power that they have over your choices, decisions and actions. Change your habits. And consider risks that might support your mindset change.

GET LOST ONCE IN A WHILE – ON PURPOSE

AT THE HEART OF our experience is loss. We do all we can to avoid it. We don't want to lose things or people and we don't like to *be* lost. To be immersed in the unfamiliar and with no idea how to get back to where we want to be, can be frightening – or a challenge. Or both.

The idea

We often believe that loss of things and getting lost are bad. And sometimes both can be, horrifically so. But rarely – and perhaps not often. There are benefits in losing ourselves, our bearings and our direction. When we're lost, our senses are heightened. We're more alert, more aware and more liable to address the immediate moment, circumstances and environment. We have to put everything else on hold until we've sorted out the problem. It's a mindset focus.

In 1963, W. Whittaker was the first American to climb Everest despite running out of oxygen along the way. The explorer later became CEO of Recreational Equipment Inc. While nobody wants to get lost on a mountain, Whittaker advocated taking new hiking routes whilst being alert to any dangers. Once we've lost yourself, we enter into that state of vulnerability, acceptance, understanding and even awakening. And maybe panic. We learn to cope and (usually) manage our fears.

Richard Branson welcomes the occasional 'getting lost'. "My favorite mode of transport is hot-air ballooning ," Branson told *The Wall Street Journal* recently. "It's so graceful to be blown by the wind, to go where the wind takes you." But he's 100 per cent aware that balloons get lost and that's part of the positive adventure, not negative disaster. But he prepared and that's a clue to 'getting lost' success. Because he knew little about ballooning, Branson trained for three years. On all of his record attempts, he has faced disaster and possible death. That's not necessarily what getting lost means and Branson recognizes that his ballooning helped make Virgin a global brand, but he's rejected the idea that he did anything for any reason other than pure joy and curiosity.

It can be difficult to think rationally when we're lost. It's an exercise in using our problem-solving capacity and initiative. Also, being or feeling like an outsider from time-to-time is important because it changes the way we see and treat others, particularly where we for once are in the minority. Knowing what it's like to be stared at, misunderstood or stand out as different is a profound experience and one that many people have day after day and are never able to escape.

Being lost isn't a bad thing if we *know* we're lost and we know how to benefit from it mentally or, indeed, physically. And we're not necessarily talking about being lost with a raging torrent in front of us, a ravine behind and hungry wolves to the left and right. There's a great scene in *Butch Cassidy and the Sundance Kid* in which the two face a ravine with a fast-flowing river at the bottom and a posse behind them. Will they jump or face the posse?

Most of us consider being lost annoying, frustrating or even terrifying. We avoid being lost by using our smart phones and GPS so that we can always figure out where we are, where we're going and how to get there (and back). But being lost means we are on the threshold of an opportunity to discover something about our strength.

Mountaineer Alison Levine, author of, *On the Edge: The Art of High-Impact Leadership* knows better than most about getting lost. The former Goldman Sachs associate has conquered the highest peak on every continent and skied to both the North and South Poles all with a rare heart condition. Learning to rely on herself to survive has taught her how to succeed under any circumstances. Acclimatizing to Everest's thin air is a long and frustrating, but necessary process which means that you have to go up and then down and then up again in incremental stages. "We tend to think progress is defined by forward motion," writes Levine, "but sometimes you have to go backwards to reach your end goal. When you don't get a promotion or take a job that you feel is a step down, look at it as an opportunity to review your skills, rest up and get stronger." While we tend to reward people with perfect track records, she says, "sometimes it's the people who stumbled, who've been beaten and bruised and have taken risks that achieve the most."

Rebecca Solnit's book, *A Field Guide To Getting Lost* deals with different aspects of what a person can find out about themselves in the process. Whether it's about getting lost in the wilderness, being an immigrant, losing oneself in sex, drugs and rock and roll, the book explores the inevitability, costs and consequences of becoming lost – and the fact that we can sustain most challenges, if not all. Think about Jack Kerouac's *On The Road*. There's something inherently appealing about throwing some things into a bag and jumping into a car, setting off to you-know-not-where with no plan, trusting that ideas and adventure will find you along the way, believing that discoveries will be littered on the side of the road, waiting for you to pick them up.

The practice

- "Go somewhere you know nothing about and see what happens." Karl Ove Knausgård from his book *Min kamp 5*

- Getting lost doesn't have to take you into the middle of nowhere. In a city, you can explore many new places. At work, in a large organization, you can do the same.

- Being lost in a foreign country or strange city can be worrying. But, instead of looking at it as a potentially devastating situation, try looking at it as an opportunity to hone skills that are important to your growth. You're likely to be OK.

- Being lost is an opportunity to test your problem-solving skills. You'll not only figure out how to get back on the right track (and you will), but doing so on your own will leave you feeling like you accomplished something.

- Getting lost often makes for the best memories and stories.

LEARN FROM WHAT GOES WRONG

We have to be willing to admit to our mistakes and explain them. Things go wrong for everyone from time-to-time. Fact. How you manage and deal with these things will determine your strength of character and, in turn, the experience will hopefully strengthen your character.

The idea

In the TED Talk, *Why Good Leaders Make You Feel Safe*, leadership expert Simon Sinek examined the impact that feelings of security have on employees. He explained that when people feel safe they're likely to use their talents to support their leaders. Not least there's less toxicity. When there's a lack of security, employees are forced to expend energy to protect themselves and this leads to a weakening of the organization.

While Microsoft introduced MSN Search in 1998, the site used an existing search engine, Inktomi, to gather results. It seems all Gates' attention was focused on browsers, allowing Google to come along and become the search engine of choice. In 2009, Microsoft introduced Bing, but it never matched the popularity of Google. If we can learn anything from this, it's that we shouldn't ignore our competitors. But of course Microsoft, which used to be just a software licensing company, began making hardware with the Xbox and now builds its own Surface tablets and phone handsets. It's now a software-writing, tablet-making, phone-building company – just like Apple. By the way, Microsoft's Steve Ballmer actually laughed at the iPhone. "It doesn't appeal to business customers because it doesn't have a keyboard," he's alleged to have said.

When Ronald Johnson took the helm of failing J.C Penney in 2011, he received a warm welcome. Many were intrigued to see what the former head of retail at Apple would do. Unfortunately, a series of bad judgments followed, including firing the company's long-term ad agency, laying off many of its managers and stopping store discounts. Revenues dropped by 25 per cent in 2012 and Johnson was fired in 2013. It shows the importance of knowing your audience. Critical always. Repeated mistakes can be avoided if we learn lessons from the first mistake – in Johnson's case by perhaps establishing focus groups, speaking with his customer base and keeping communication open to see how customers would react to big changes before making them.

In 2012, Apple launched its iOS 6 Maps, riddled with bugs: inaccurate location placement and satellite imagery, poor transit directions and weak connections with third-party routing apps. While software bugs are normal at launch, offering the app in that state caused confusion for users and left many at Apple red-faced, with the blame falling on Cook who did analyze what was wrong and rectified the issues – fast.

It's always a risk to consider what went wrong with something that's happened to us because we may not want to admit any fault – and therefore we don't. Analysis becomes a risk in our mind's eye and therefore we avoid it. The tendency is to blame circumstances on bad luck – or on someone else.

Not all mistakes are ours to control. But, when they are, we must face up to the fact. Part of improving our mindset involves coping with life's stresses. Acknowledging errors is important. Richard Branson made an error of judgement with Virgin Cola. It didn't sell globally. He wrote, "As for what lost the most money, probably Virgin Cola. It is still No 1 in Bangladesh though."

In 1997, Apple was days from bankruptcy. Steve Jobs came back, used his industry connections (particularly Bill Gates) to get the company stable and began growth. The iPod, originally conceived as a device to make people buy more Macintosh computers, instead turned into a huge product line. But by 2005, Jobs recognized that making iPods wouldn't be enough: phones would be able to store as much music as an iPod. So, Apple made a phone that did everything – and that saved the business. And then some.

The reason Blackberry worked was because iPhone and Android just weren't there in the early and mid 2000s. In 2012, Blackberry CEO Thorsten Heins needed to turn the firm's fortunes around after sales dwindled. Instead of investing though, he cut costs and streamlined the organization that had grown huge under the two previous CEOs. He also placed the entire company's future on BlackBerry 10 phones, which were late to market and didn't perform as well as their competitors'. A poor plan and a worse reputation were the final blows to Thorsten Heins' reign.

The practice

- Failure and fault are virtually inseparable in most households, organizations and cultures. Children learn that admitting failure means taking the blame. We all make bad decisions and mistakes or, better put, we make some that don't work. We need to learn from them.

- It's easy to become a victim of oversight, carelessness, misinformation, misunderstanding, manipulation, impulse or another negative influencing factor. Understand why you did what you did or why what happened did happen.

- Test an idea before going 'public'.

- If you make a mistake, take a moment to regulate your body (and that means managing your breathing, tears and agitation) after which consider what happened. Maybe you were at fault. Maybe not. Everything has consequences. Decide how to respond.

- Forgive yourself.

- Remember, the past is behind you and no matter how badly things went, there is nothing you can do to change them.

FIRST IMPRESSIONS DON'T ALWAYS COUNT

It's said that we make up our minds about meeting someone new within seconds. Sure, we change our view of people as time goes on, but we do become fixed in our views probably too soon and too often. When it comes to the decision-making process, arbitrary factors can often get in the way and can lead to confused and muddled thinking.

The idea

The ability to judge others is linked to our instinct for self-preservation, which tells us almost instantly whether someone is a friend or a foe, a threat or an ally. Before there's been any time for reflection, we decide if the person is attractive, physically acceptable, friendly or hostile. Our opinion develops from the emotion that this meeting arouses. The judgement is almost instant. But can we trust these snap judgements?

"Research has found that first impressions are surprisingly valid," writes Daniel Kahneman, psychologist, Nobel laureate and author of *Thinking, Fast And Slow*. "However, first impressions are not perfect and making a quick decision about someone can have consequences. If your first impression is a mistake, it can take a while to realise this, as your expectations tend to be self-fulfilling. When you expect a certain reaction, you are likely to perceive it even if it isn't there." That's why it's important, when making these judgements, that we do not allow our assumptions and fixed beliefs to take over. Growth mindset thinking should be clear on that.

Our brain makes a judgement in a tenth of a second when it sees a new face, according to a study led by the Princeton University psychologist Alex Todorov. He writes, "... the reason we trust first impressions automatically is that they feel right. The reason we're often wrong is that these impressions are not accurate as inferences of character... But obviously that judgement would be a poor predictor of how a person is across time and situations." He believes that people never rigorously test their hunches. He also thinks that our misguided first impressions are becoming more important in the digital world. He has written, "Different images of the same person can generate completely different impressions. The person can look attractive and competent in one image and silly and not very smart in another."

Most of us aren't even aware that we're constantly making snap judgements on individuals. Instinct is nature's way of helping us make the right choices and to protect us, but the reality is that it can often be a mistake to make instant decisions. It's easy to judge people on what we assume. And that might be related to a fixed rather than a growth mindset.

The practice

- Why do first impressions matter to you? Because initially, it's all you have to go on. It's a starting point; nothing more.

- We tend to size each other up quickly. Even if you're presented with evidence to the contrary, you're attached to your initial impressions of people – which is why you should be aware of the impression *you* make on others.

- A first impression is your initial condition for analyzing another person, but be open-minded because your first impression may be incorrect. We're subject to cognitive bias that distorts our judgement.

- Be aware of any prejudices and issues you have about colour, religion, ethnicity, education, accent and background. You should be moderating and reconsidering your views anyway.

GET EXCITED ABOUT ALL THE POSSIBILITIES AHEAD

LOOKING FORWARD TO THINGS is natural. The adrenalin of excitement makes us feel full of zest and it's right to look for opportunities about which to get excited. Should mindset change be exciting? It should. Is it exciting and risky? Of course. All change is risky and much of it is exciting.

The idea

New possibilities can be scary. Warren Buffet wrote, "It takes twenty years to build a reputation and five minutes to ruin it. If you think about that, you'll do things differently." Buffett has the ability to analyze the value of a business and its potential including risk and possibilities. He invests in people who understand the importance of upholding ethics and of having long-term goals. About possibilities Mark Cuban (owner of Dallas Mavericks, co-owner of 2929 Entertainment and chairman of AXS TV) writes that, "There are no shortcuts: you have to work hard and try to put yourself in a position where, if luck strikes, you can see the opportunity and take advantage of it."

Mindset change is hopefully a probability for you but not a definite. It's hard to embrace uncertainty. Sometimes all we can see is a cloud of doubt. But, look at it differently – when the future isn't fixed, we can become and do anything within our (current or newly developed) abilities. Passion comes into this. Passion equals excitement and excitement gets the blood racing.

When we set a goal, we don't feel like we have to work on it. We *get* to work on it – a huge difference. Speaking to Reuters at a 2017 Web Summit in Lisbon, Carlos Ghosn, CEO of Renault-Nissan, said the extra two hours – the average daily time spent by drivers behind the wheel worldwide – will open an entire new world of technological possibilities. "The most exciting technology is the combination of connected (cars) and autonomous (driving)," Ghosn told Reuters. "Now the car becomes a mobile space, connected, where you can have a video conference, see a movie, talk to your kids or consult your doctor."

Look at another sector. While the word telemedicine was once considered a catch-all term for any type of healthcare service administered remotely, over the last decade it has been applied to a myriad of virtual care services, tools and companies. Scott Decker, CEO of telemedicine platform provider MDLive, believes that the main macro-level challenges affecting the telemedicine industry are the same as those in traditional healthcare, with cost barriers and a lack of primary care providers. From there, he says, telemedicine companies can rise up to expand the ideas people have around how to manage their wellness. He believes that telemedicine will increase exponentially worldwide over the next ten years.

Ripple's CEO, Brad Garlinghouse, has produced the fourth-most-valuable cryptocurrency XRP. That currency is now worth almost $9 billion. Lest you're lost, a cryptocurrency is a digital asset designed to work as a medium of exchange using cryptography to secure the transactions. The term 'wire transfer' dates back to the 1800s. It's based on an antiquated system. The friction of moving value remains surprisingly high. Garlinghouse believes that cryptocurrencies will become super popular. XRP was built to solve a payments problem. And it's a much more Internet-ready process. It's faster and more accurate than the current SWIFT system. It allows banks to transfer money with each other and settle transactions in seconds versus days. The cost to do that is lower too and process visibility is high. Today, we can send transfers, but there's no tracking number for that transaction, although we expect on-demand alerts of what's happening. So, Ripple (and others) sell their software to banks to send and receive in real-time on a massive scale.

Google's Larry Page has commented that, "Lots of companies don't succeed over time. What do they fundamentally do wrong? They usually miss the future." Similar to businesses thinking it's okay to take their foot off the gas pedal, many brands get stuck in useless business practices, ultimately hurting their possibilities of growth and invention through their own mistakes.

Life is an adventure with twists and turns, some we know, some we know nothing about and some we possibly imagine. Our excitement about our lives emerges as we gain a deeper capacity to accept things as they are now. That doesn't mean that we should stop planning and wanting to do better or to change. It does mean though that it's easy to fall into worrying about an issue or conjuring up a worst-case scenario. Remember, if the glass is half-empty, then it's also already half-full.

The practice

- Brexit, de-globalization, cyber security, the rise of machines and so on all have an upside. You mustn't lose the childlike wonder about looking forward to possibilities. In order to prevent ourselves from being disappointed, we sometimes limit the anticipation. But that's a negative and isn't going to boost our mindset. Look for possibilities. Some will work, some won't. But look for them.

- Instead of relying on others to make your life exciting, rely on you. You're the only person you know who will always be there, no matter what. Get excited about all the possibilities ahead; you can't control the future, but you do have the ability to shape it.

- Visualize a successful outcome to anything you're doing or planning. When's the last time you asked yourself, "What's the *best* thing that can happen?"

- Teach yourself to see other side of a problem, possibility or situation.

TAKE COURAGE

Courage is the ability to face our fears and try something different or maybe intimidating. It usually needs us to go out of our comfort zone and fear invariably stops us doing that. But courage is an essential part of managing change and of having a growth mindset.

The idea

Courage is something that everybody wants – an attribute of good character that makes us worthy of respect. Global cultures are rich with tales of bravery and self-sacrifice for the greater good. Courage isn't just physical bravery. Social activists, such as Martin Luther King, showed courage. Successful entrepreneurs who take financial risks to follow their dreams exemplify the rewards that courage can bring.

Software consultancy ThoughtWorks reported that the best business leaders share an approach to the running of their organizations that could be termed as 'courage'. The report, *The Next Big Disruption: Courageous Executives* profiles a segment of international leaders: 87 per cent of targeted top 500 executives agreed that being courageous is necessary to achieve goals and maintain a strong competitive advantage.

Courage is not the same as confidence. Confidence is the feeling or belief that we can have faith in someone or something. Courage is our ability to do something that normally frightens us; its strength in the face of adversity.

Confidence and courage aren't magic. They're built. Other people can help us develop courage, or indeed confidence, but the doing part can only ever be down to us – you or me. Courage is our ability to act in the face of legitimate fears and grows only with effort. So, if courage is built, then something else is true: to act with restraint and fear does not make anyone a permanent coward. Steve Jobs wasn't a coward when the chips were down. He introduced products, services and entire business models completely unlike anything in existence. He disdained market testing (thus keeping his plans secret) and couldn't be sure he would succeed – and he risked significant losses and ridicule if he failed.

Brave managers keep making value–creating investments in uncertain times. DuPont maintained R&D spending even through the Great Depression, inventing nylon, neoprene and other products that would earn billions for decades thereafter. "But this is how I've always done it," people say to justify their aversion to change. How it's always been done might no longer be the best way to do whatever 'it' is. Sometimes the bravest thing we can do is to call it a day, learn the lessons and move on. Whether it's standing out, speaking up or owning mistakes, courage doesn't guarantee success; it might precede it. It takes courage to discover who we really are and to follow our convictions. We're inculcated with beliefs from an early age about who we should be and the direction we should take in life. It can be scary to live on our own terms and do things differently – to change beliefs – but that's what a growth mindset involves.

The practice

- Without courage, you can't make a difference and without confidence you can't make it happen.

- You don't have to be a hero to be courageous. Everyday courage comes from embracing struggles and uncertainties that you may encounter every week.

- When you display courage, you're taking a risk and admitting that something could go wrong with that risk. That's the nature of 'risk'.

- Displaying courage doesn't mean that you're invincible. It's common to display courage and still have self-doubt.

37 DON'T FEAR FAILURE

MARK ZUCKERBERG WROTE, "THE biggest risk is not taking any risk... In a world that's changing really quickly, the only strategy that is guaranteed to fail is not taking risks." Yes, we tend to view risk-taking negatively and fear failure – often regarding risk and even opportunity as dangerous and even unwise. But while some risks certainly don't pay off, it's important to remember that some do. Failure is part of risk-taking, but it shouldn't be feared; that way lies taking no risk. Drew Houston, Dropbox CEO: "Don't worry about failure; you only have to be right once."

The idea

Apple's Tim Cook wrote, "We change every day. We changed every day when Steve was here and we've been changing every day since he's not been here. We don't fear it. The core and the values in the core remain the same as they were in '98, as they were in '05, as they were in '10. I don't think the values should change. But everything else can change." Possibly, you may think, easy for him to say, but the tenets hold true for us all.

Daniel Vasella, chairman of Novartis, knows like any exec in pharma, that the road to drug discovery is paved with ideas that don't work and developments that don't go anywhere. Said Vasella, "In R&D, in the beginning of our process, we lose 90 per cent of the products. When we are down the road, seven to ten years, we still lose 30 per cent of the products. There is no way around it: we succeed less often than we fail." Without those failures, however, discovery isn't possible. Again, easy for big businesses to say, but the principles apply to all of us.

Fear of failure and fear of the unknown are common, but we mustn't embrace these and use them as excuses or even reasons. All fears can freeze action or cause a retreat from objectives. Fear keeps a mindset locked in a state of helplessness. We must think of risk as an opportunity to succeed, rather than a path to failure. Thomas Edison said, "I have not failed. I've just found 10,000 ways that won't work."

Success rarely falls into our laps – we have to pursue it. Huffington Post's founder, Arianna Huffington identified the fear of failure as a roadblock to success. She has said, "We women are a little more risk-averse because whenever you launch something there's a big chance it's not going to work. And we have a bigger problem with failure... Failure isn't the end of one's journey to success, but usually the beginning. Failure is not the opposite of success but a stepping stone to success." Doing something different is uncomfortable; we don't know if it will work. But taking decisions on things with unproven results or without guarantees is the only way to create change.

The practice

- To avoid failure, prepare endlessly and sit through meetings, pore over data, think about what ifs. Planning is good, but then you have to press the button and 'do'.

- The only real failure is failing to fail. Without a few failures under your belt, you haven't really stretched yourself.

- Failure has to be tackled head-on – not avoided, but explored. Then it's not scary.

- Wrote author and musician Eloise Ristad, "When we give ourselves permission to fail, we, at the same time, give ourselves permission to excel." Good advice.

38 | UNCERTAINTY IS FINE

MOST PEOPLE FIND GREAT discomfort in uncertainty. Uncertainty and mystery are energies of life. Don't let them scare you unduly – and with a growth mindset they won't, for they will spark creativity and positivity.

The idea

Many of the key assumptions we make in business, politics, leadership, morals and the economy are being challenged. Liann Eden, founding partner of managing consultants Eden McCallum, comments, "Managing uncertainty is just the new normal. We tend to focus on Brexit and Trump, but before that a lot of businesses worried about... interest rates and changes in income costs."

Staying on top of uncertainty is as much about planning for failure as it is about hoping for the best. Experts at handling uncertainty aren't afraid to admit that they could be wrong – and that allows them to make contingency plans before action. Successful people know they aren't always going to make the right decisions. A recent survey by Ernst & Young declared that 90 per cent of business leaders viewed uncertainty as an opportunity for growth.

Management specialist, Peter Drucker: "The entrepreneur always searches for change, responds to it and exploits it as an opportunity." If we only sit in the safety of what we know, we will never grow. Uncertainty isn't an enemy out to shoot us, but can be an ally to push us forward. The experience of failing is more valuable than no experience at all. Henry Ford said, "Failure is simply the opportunity to begin again, this time with more intelligence." And "businesses must learn to balance the need for a more reactive, short-term focus with the need for informed, long-term strategies," wrote Elon Musk.

Uncertainty can be many things: fear-invoking, unnerving, confidence-building and empowering. It can produce results. The process of uncertainty is called life. If we knew what to expect at all times, we'd get bored. Of course, there are plenty of areas and terrible scenarios where we don't welcome uncertainty. New York City mayor Bill de Blasio's recently expressed certainty, before a January storm, that New York would witness the "biggest snowstorm in the history of this city." Predictions ranged from thirty to eight inches of snow, but de Blasio focused on the worst scenario and ignored the range of possibilities. The hours leading up to what ended up being a normal winter snowfall were marked by anxious preparations. Schools, stores, roads and the subway were closed. The storm wasn't a storm. So, New York's leaders had undermined the credibility of warnings of future disasters and New Yorkers are likely to be more sceptical of future warnings. The dilemma is this: Is it better to err on the side of caution or action? If we cry 'wolf' will people eventually take no notice?

Well, for thousands of years, the ancient Polynesians were put to the test as they navigated the uncertainty of the oceans – braving sea storms, cyclones, tides and dangerous fish. With no instruments at their disposal, they developed a great sense of their surroundings and a highly tuned intuition to read the oceans and weather. Leading through uncertainty is about building the resilience of a team and making hard decisions with limited information. Winston Churchill's leadership style was one that relied heavily on inspiration through a focus on purpose. He led in a period of huge uncertainty and, while it frightened people, with his encouragement it also galvanized them. For Churchill, uncertainty didn't result in indecision. His leadership was flawed but he had the courage to make decisions with imperfect information.

Michael Brooks in *At the Edge of Uncertainty: 11 Discoveries Taking Science by Surprise*, writes, "The edge of uncertainty is not a static line, but a dynamic, ever-changing set of answers. What other way is there for humans to behave than to push at the boundaries of our knowledge and our existence – even if the act of pushing exposes our ignorance?"

Whenever we form expectations, we're setting ourselves up for disappointment. We can guide our futures to a degree, but we can't control the outcome. If you expect the worst, you'll probably feel too negative to see and seize opportunities. If you expect the best, and with a positive mindset, you're likely to plan for what you think will probably happen.

The practice

- Don't fear uncertainty. Uncertainty has been a fact of life forever. But there are times when it heightens and we go into unknown territory e.g. The Ice Age, The Plague, the World Wars, disasters, other wars, financial crashes, weather and so on.

- Uncertainty is normal. To adapt fast, we must borrow from the Polynesians' ability to go into unchartered waters.

- If ever you think you've created a controllable, predictable life for yourself, that's an illusion. Nothing stays the same forever.

- As we face uncertainty, our brains make us overreact. Successful people are able to override this mechanism and shift their thinking in a rational direction.

- When uncertainty makes a decision difficult, it's easy to feel as if *everything* is uncertain, but that's rarely the case.

39 THINK OUTSIDE OF THE BOX

THINKING OUTSIDE THE BOX means that you leave all your experiences and attitudes behind and start to view things from a completely different perspective – unfiltered, unbiased and open. Boxes represent conventional thinking; they're assumptions that confine our creativity and ability to see new options.

The idea

Some assumptions are of course necessary. We can't make it through a day without assuming the traffic light will turn green or that our chair will support us when we sit down. But when assumptions become rigid (or, like a box, closed), they can keep us from seeing new possibilities or perspectives. And we can only think outside our box if we're positive and our minds open. Thinking outside the box implies that we don't persist with a set opinion. Sounds simple, but people do stubbornly persist with a fixed opinion, even if they know that they're mistaken – but that's also an ego thing which needs putting to one side

Thinking outside the box is more than just a business cliché. It means approaching problems in new, innovative ways, conceptualizing problems differently and understanding our position in relation to any situation in a way we'd never thought of before. There was a time when the Motorola Razr was considered a super phone. Its main feature was that it was thin. If we continued down that route, our phones would now be paper thin, but all they would be able to do is make calls. Then Apple thought outside the box. And Airbnb didn't reach mainstream success until after the company released a marketing video that answered questions about the business and put potential customers at ease. Amazon's customer focus is one of the most well-known strategies, but CEO Jeff Bezos thinks it's important to think out of the box on a regular basis. He's known to leave an empty chair at meetings, the idea being that it represents the customer – as he says, "The most important person in the room."

Galileo Galilei is a wonderful example of a person who questioned the status quo of the 'fact' that the sun revolved around the earth – prevalent as a total belief at the time. Not only did he not accept the unquestioned 'fact', but he also questioned something for which he knew the consequences of so doing. Think about that.

The practice

- From time to time, choose to meet people who work completely outside of your world. They will enable you to see new angles.

- Real creativity is usually about combining two existing ideas to make a new one. Steve Jobs said, "Creativity is simply connecting things."

- Ask a child how s/he might tackle a problem. The idea isn't to do what the child says necessarily, but to push your own thinking into an unconventional path.

- If you aren't willing to try, you won't find a solution, ever.

- Learn about how things are done in other industries. You might find that problems faced by people in other industries are similar to the problems in your own, but that they've developed really quite different ways of dealing with them.

40 AVOID TOXIC PEOPLE

THERE ARE TOXIC PEOPLE about – in all walks of life and everywhere. They act out the victim, bully, perfectionist or martyr. They may be psychotic. Their effect on any healthy growth mindset can be hugely damaging.

The idea

Recent research from the Department of Biological and Clinical Psychology at Friedrich Schiller University in Germany found that exposure to stimuli that cause strong negative emotions – the same kind of exposure we get when dealing with toxic people – caused subjects to have a massive stress response. Toxic (mostly psychotic or sociopathic) people can cause huge damage, sometimes permanent.

Leadership scholar, Jean Lipman-Blumen, defines toxic leaders as those whose, "destructive behaviors and dysfunctional personal characteristics generate serious and enduring poisonous effects...on those they lead." It's common for people with toxic behaviour to create drama in their lives, to manipulate others, to use others to meet their needs, to be hypercritical of anyone and anything, to be jealous, to bemoan their bad fortune and others' good luck and to be violent. We might possibly consider Dennis Kozlowski, CEO of Tyco who was sent to prison for massive fraud, Jeffrey Skilling, Chairman at Enron Corporation who was sentenced to 24 years in prison, Kenneth Lay also of Enron, Robert Rubin, Chairman at Goldman Sachs, Robert Maxwell, Zynga CEO Mark Pincus, film producer Scott Rudin, MTV Founder and Clear Channel CEO Robert Pittman – and one could go on. People who prey off the energy of others are often charismatic. They are controlling and often head up a gang of acolytes – and they are by no means all famous. They are global and can inhabit any organization.

According to Miguel López, director of Franklin Covey, Costa Rica, it's necessary for top management to prioritize these people who become harmful and manage the situation very fast. But that doesn't happen often by any means. Sociopaths are invariably high-performing superstars, using their charisma to ingratiate themselves with people who matter. But, if anyone is singled out as a target they won't stop until they've dealt with that person, feeling no empathy whatsoever.

Michigan Governor, Rick Snyder and his team sparked national outrage in the U.S. after an attempt at cost-savings left the impoverished city of Flint with a lead-tainted water supply that was blamed for illness and brain damage, especially among children. Called to testify before Congress, Snyder labelled the experience the most humbling of his life – then attempted to shift blame. He called it "a failure of government" and blasted the Environmental Protection Agency for its "dumb and dangerous" rules on allowable amounts of lead in the water. Here's another example. Martin Winterkorn, Volkswagen's CEO, led VW during the disastrous scandal as company engineers installed software that manipulated emissions on about 11 million diesel vehicles. Winterkorn claimed ignorance. Critics were sceptical, given that he is known as a micro-manager. Then there's the fact that the company acknowledged that a warning of potential wrongdoing was sent to him.

The practice

- Distance yourself from toxic people.

- Seek help and support. You might read *The Evil Executive* by Simon Maier.

- It's easy to say it's all the other person's fault, but there are two sides to every coin. Are you contributing to the toxic behaviour? Are you being pulled into a downward emotional spiral? Be positive and remove yourself from this person's influence.

- Chances are you aren't going to change this person, so your best bet is to focus on what you can control. That may mean leaving.

- Toxic people in any scenario can spread negativity like wildfire. The more positive you are, the better.

CHAPTER 5
BE NICE TO YOU

REMIND YOURSELF OF YOUR BLESSINGS

People often forget what they have – and search for what they haven't. That search can be debilitating because it might be unachievable. While setting yourself targets is critical for growth, it's also important for your peace of mind to remind yourself of what you already have in your life.

The idea

Uruguay's former president, Jose 'Pepe' Mujica, was dubbed the world's poorest president. A former Tupamaros guerrilla fighter in the 1960s and '70s, Mujica was shot many times and spent 14 years in jail. When he was elected Uruguayan president in 2009, he donated 90 per cent of his presidential salary to charity and refused the presidential palace, preferring his modest farm. He often said that he was grateful for what he had and had no desire to focus on what he could have.

Some people expect or wait for a better future. Or spend time regretting the past. They're waiting to be happier. The present is where things for which we should be grateful sit. Of course, you could list all the things you *don't* have. Or you could put those very same things as your goals.

In the movie, *It's a Wonderful Life*, George Bailey had to see a world without him in it to appreciate all the wonders of his life. Although most of us haven't missed a flight that wound up crashing or had an angel help us see our wonderful lives, we've passed a collision on the road and realised it could have been us or heard about someone diagnosed with a disease and had a moment of thanks for our own health. Even something as trivial as thinking we forgot our keys, only to find them in a different pocket, can elicit a real sense of relief and appreciation.

CEO of global investment banking firm Jefferies Group, Rich Handler and Chairman Brian Friedman sent an open letter to their staff expressing what they were grateful for in 2016. Interestingly the tone is one of overall thanks: "This is the beginning of the season where we remind ourselves of our blessings and all we have to be thankful for in our lives." In particular, the executives were thankful for, "free speech, the pursuit of happiness, checks and balances and the peaceful transition of rule." Their missive included everything for which there should be current gratitude.

Lindsay Avner, founder of cancer charity Bright Pink writes that, "... I have the opportunity to wake up every day and have a profound sense of meaning in purpose. I am thankful to work in the area of prevention and early detection, to have the chance to help young women understand their breast and ovarian cancer risk and do something about it. I am thankful for the countless lives we have saved through education, support, prevention and early detection."

Lorna Borenstein, founder and CEO of Grokker, writes, "Every day, no matter how long or trying, has its small joys – a cup of coffee from a smiling barista, a colleague calling your efforts out in a meeting, a funny meme from your brother – are all tiny beads of joy you can string together. In fact, joy is as essential to a healthy life as exercise and good nutrition; it's fuel for the soul... So place a bright yellow sticky note in your work area that says "What are you grateful for today?" and answer it as often as you can."

We do sometimes take things for granted. Despite our own choice of creating a busy (and therefore a possibly stressful) lifestyle, ironically, we constantly complain about how stressful and tiresome our lives actually are. It's a nonsensical badge of 'courage' to moan because we can then ignore the good things. And notice them when they're gone.

The practice

- Remind yourself that you're unique and one of a kind. Don't think of yourself as a nobody, that you have little value. Remember that that you probably already achieved (and have) a great deal.

- Count your blessings, not your troubles.

- We are too busy, too preoccupied. But you have to be still sometimes and smile at what you have in your life..

- Accepting the fact that life is imperfect gives you enough space to expect it to be hard sometimes.

- Nothing wastes more energy than worrying. We all do it. Worrying is a complete waste of energy.

- Take time to smell the flowers.

TAKE TIME OUT TO THINK

To GROW, YOU MUST ponder, toss around ideas, think. Take time out to just look about you more, really see what's going on, absorb it and think about what you're seeing. Really think.

The idea

In 2011, when Jack Dorsey was running Twitter and Square full-time, he said that, to get everything done, he gave each day a theme. This allowed him to recall and refocus on the day's task once distractions were out of the way. He took Saturday off to hike and spend Sunday focusing on reflections, feedback, strategy, getting ready for the rest of the week. But mostly thinking.

Instead of watching reality television, we can seek out the reality of the world around us – the unexplored or even the already explored. Even looking again at things that we know well can bring new understanding. This isn't as airy fairy as it may sound either. Really looking and really being aware can heighten our senses and make us slow down a little to consider life and what's important and what is less so. It helps us to manage problems.

Reed Hastings, Netflix's CEO, says that he takes six weeks' vacation a year because it's important for work-life balance. He's also said, "It is helpful. You often do your best thinking when you're off hiking in some mountain or something. You get a different perspective on things." And Richard Branson wrote, "Maintaining focus on having fun isn't just about rest and recuperation: When you go on vacation, your routine is interrupted; the places you go and the new people you meet can inspire you in unexpected ways. As an entrepreneur or business leader, if you didn't come back from your vacation with some ideas about how to shake things up, it's time to consider making some changes."

AOL CEO Tim Armstrong, for instance, makes his executives spend 10 per cent of their day or four hours per week, just thinking. Jeff Weiner, CEO of LinkedIn, schedules two hours of uninterrupted thinking time every day. Jack Dorsey walks a lot and thinks. Bill Gates takes a week off twice a year just to reflect deeply without interruption.

The way we perceive ourselves in relation to the rest of the world influences our behaviours and our beliefs. The dynamics of psychology – cognition, perception, learning, emotion, attitudes and relationships – play a role in how we see ourselves and our environments. And by the word 'environment' this can mean anywhere – home, a long way from home, new places, old places, on holiday.

The practice
- Take time off for thinking.

- Put time in your diary for thinking.

- Don't feel guilty for taking walks in the park or having a coffee while others are in the office.

- Explore museums or galleries and really focus on what you see. Small, bite-sized pieces at a time is the rule of thumb. Really understand something about the pictures, their back stories and the artists.

- Aim for shorter meetings and cut down your to-do list for the week

WHAT A DAY FOR
A DAYDREAM

WE ARE TAUGHT THAT when we let our minds wander we should feel some guilt. It's not a skill we're encouraged to develop. Regardless of what we do for a living, all of us are faced with issues that we haven't encountered before and for which we need to find unique solutions. Daydreaming is good for you. When we daydream, we can lose ourselves in a self-generated flow of consciousness. We can do anything, go anywhere within the privacy of our minds.

The idea

Daydreaming can help positivity and create a better 'can do' attitude. It's a means by which to escape the outer world, to face our fears, to entertain ourselves and to explore our ideas. But those who like to indulge in reverie are often negatively labelled dreamers, dawdlers, idle or unfocussed. Not so. When we consider that we live in a consumer-based world that worships productivity and efficiency, it's no wonder that daydreaming is seen in a negative light, as a lazy habit, a waste of time and a distraction. Sigmund Freud declared daydreaming to be a sign of mental illness, a neurotic and infantile tendency indulged by those who were unfulfilled.

After he was expelled from school for rebelling against rote learning, Einstein is believed to have begun his theory of relativity while he daydreamed about running beside a sunbeam to the edge of the universe. Newton developed his theory of gravity after he saw an apple fall from a tree while daydreaming. Sir Paul McCartney has admitted that some of the Beatles' most popular work was literally 'dreamt up'.

Daydreaming (using the mind to distance ourselves from the present moment) and mindfulness (immersing ourselves in the present moment), contribute to a healthy mindset – the better we get at both, the better we become at filtering out distraction. Much of our world is automated and we are constantly flooded with external distraction, so the ability to daydream is important. Today it's so easy to turn to our phones to fill in the blank periods and that stops the mind wandering.

According to Washington University neurologist Marcus E. Raichle, "When you don't use a muscle, that muscle really isn't doing much of anything... But when your brain is supposedly doing nothing and daydreaming, it's really doing a tremendous amount. We call it 'resting state,' but the brain isn't resting at all." Gunnar Engellau, Volvo's president in the 1950s hired an engineer named Nils Bohlin to make cars safer – not just their cars, but *all* cars. Recognizing the need for a device that absorbed force across both the chest and waist, Bohlin developed the three-point seatbelt that's in every vehicle. He came up with the idea while walking.

Daydreaming is associated with creativity – our most creative and inventive moments can come when daydreaming. It's also an escape and allows us to think of risk and 'what if' scenarios.

The practice

- Daydreams reveal desire. The desire becomes intention. Intention turns into a plan. A plan sets goals.

- Daydreaming supports your creativity and could be the start of great ideas. Almost all of your ambitions start life as daydreams.

- While your physical self is in the present, your mind can skip into the past or future at any time you want.

- Daydreaming has a learning function. When you daydream about things that have already happened, you review the events and think about alternatives.

- Daydreaming helps us rehearse.

44 LISTEN PROPERLY

According to the International Listening Association, only about 50 per cent of what we hear is retained immediately after we hear it and only 20 per cent after that. Listening is crucial to growth and learning.

The idea

Churchill wrote, "Courage is what it takes to stand up and speak; courage is also what it takes to sit down and listen." Ralph G. Nichols, author of *Are You Listening?* wrote, "The most basic of all human needs is the need to understand and be understood. The best way to understand people is to listen to them." In today's high-speed world, communication is more important than ever, yet we seem to devote less and less time to really listening to one another.

Genuine listening has become rare. But that shouldn't be the case. Listening builds relationships and ensures understanding. Careful listening equals fewer errors, better problem solving and less time wasted. Listening is an active process by which we make sense of, assess and respond to that which we hear. The people who really listen to us are the ones we move towards because we like to be properly listened to.

In 2012, Kevin Sharer, Amgen's CEO said in a McKinsey interview, "For most of my career, I was an awful listener in almost every possible way... The best advice I ever heard about listening – advice that significantly changed my own approach – came from Sam Palmisano, when he was talking to our leadership team. Someone asked him why his experience working in Japan was so important to his leadership development, and he said, 'Because I learned to listen.' And I thought, 'That's pretty amazing.' He also said, 'I learned to listen by having only one objective: comprehension.' ... Listening for comprehension helps you get that information, of course, but it's more than that: it's also the greatest sign of respect you can give someone."

Most of us really don't listen very well. Or, if we do manage to listen, we are often just waiting until the other person finishes so we can say what's on our minds. And that's not really listening. Over time, the result of this is that we disregard what others say and we don't properly assimilate what we're being told. Then we don't understand others' concerns because we don't listen. All of us want to be listened to and all of us want to be heard. In *Don't Sweat the Small Stuff*, psychotherapist Richard Carlson, gives us the context: "We often treat communication as if it were a race. It's almost like our goal is to have no time gaps between the conclusion of the sentence of the person we are speaking with and the beginning of our own. If you think about it, you'll notice that it takes an enormous amount of energy and is very stressful to be sitting at the edge of your seat trying to guess what the person in front of you (or on the telephone) is going to say so that you can fire back your response. But as you wait for the people you are communicating with to finish, as you simply listen more intently to what is being said, you'll notice that the pressure you feel is off."

Listening is obviously not limited to speech. Listening to music can enhance our mood and performance. Whether we're performing it or listening to it, music can increase our happiness (as well as the happiness of those around us.) Music can lift the spirits. As we listen, music works on the autonomic nervous system, responsible for controlling blood pressure and heartbeat, as well as the limbic system, which is responsible for feelings and emotions. Listening to music during exercise can help to release endorphins – to increase endurance, boost mood and offer a distraction. Listening to the radio, listening to the dialogue of a movie, a TV programme or a play – all require focus and attention. Focus is key to a growth mindset and the benefit of really listening is clarity and... focus.

The practice

- Authentic listening generates respect and trust between talker and listener. Employees (or indeed partners) will respond better to managers (or partners) whom they think are listening properly.

- In most cultures, eye contact (in face to face scenarios) is considered a basic ingredient of effective communication.

- The important thing is to be attentive.

- Listen without judging the other person or mentally criticizing the things s/he tells you.

- Don't be a sentence-grabber, i.e. don't finish people's sentences. It's bloody annoying.

- Don't interrupt with what you want to say.

- Don't think of what you're going to say next and not listen. That's bloody rude.

- Listening requires patience.

45 LAUGH

LAUGHING IS GOOD FOR US. It's relaxing. It makes us feel at one with the world – and feeling at one with the world is always going to help you dismiss negativity and encourage positivity. Laughter is a leveller and puts any negative stuff into context.

The idea

Between all the violence, trauma and hostility in our world – as well as the constant news cycle and perpetual connectivity of social media, we're exposed to a stream of horrifying images and negative information. We're no longer just informed about what's happening (if it's all to be believed). Instead, we're often watching it happen, sometimes in real time and repeatedly. So how do we balance our desire to confront the reality of the world with the need to take care of our mindset? Should we click on that link showing the hurricane, the gunfire or the evil? Should we have a balance of some kind?

Do you remember the last time you really laughed? At a joke, a story, a memory, a situation, a film. Laughing so hard that you felt that you couldn't catch your breath? Or just chuckling and grinning. Laughing makes us feel good. Feeling good about yourself and all around you – even if not permanently – is absolutely essential for mindset change and uplifted spirits. "There is little success where there is little laughter," wrote Scottish-American industrialist Andrew Carnegie. NASA has publicly stated that when the space agency recruits future astronauts one of the personality traits they will be looking for is humour, believing that candidates who demonstrate a sense of humour are more flexible, more creative and better able to deal with stress.

Laughing lowers blood pressure. By reducing the level of stress hormones, we're reducing anxiety. Laughter is also a bit of a cardio workout. Endorphins are the body's natural painkillers and, by laughing, we can release endorphins. Laughter can also increase our overall sense of well-being and ability to relate to others. American author and CBS news journalist, Eric Sevareid, wrote, "Next to power without honor, the most dangerous thing in the world is power without humor." That needs qualifying – grisly humour and humour at others' expense are unacceptable.

"People don't buy from clowns." The quote from advertising pioneer Claude C. Hopkins may have been true in 1923, but times have certainly changed. Some of the biggest brands in the world use humour to sell their products on social media. Humour allows us to showcase the more relatable, human side of brands. Virgin America did this well for example on their Instagram page featuring their staff in comedic situations on holiday.

The practice

- Making people laugh has the potential to make you feel better.

- Laughter is contagious.

- Laughter bonds and makes us feel involved.

- Practice safe humour that builds rather than divides relationships, that laughs *with* people, not *at* people.

- Offensive humour – such as sexist or racist jokes – is strictly off-limits. Ditto sarcastic or bullying humour.

46 TAKE A BREAK FROM THE NEWS

We've just mentioned news. News is often depressing. Take time off from the news. It doesn't mean that you don't care, but it does mean that you can focus on yourself and issues close to you.

The idea

In a TED Talk: *Information is Food,* journalist JP Rangaswami compared eating McDonald's for 31 days, as in *Supersize Me*, to watching Fox News for 31 days. In essence, mainstream news is the fast food of information. There are much healthier types of information we can and should consume.

History has its place of course and can help us understand issues and perhaps help predict the future, but too much focus can leave us bored or overwhelmed. The historian Michael Beschloss recalls that after President Kennedy spoke to the U.S. about the Cuban missile crisis, in October 1962, "the networks immediately went back to their normal programming." Today, he says, "pundits comment immediately on Presidential speeches – and cable news dissects the speech for hours."

News is everywhere – on TV, in newspapers, via tweets, Instagram, emails, the radio – and 24/7. Some of the news is false and some poorly reported. Some will trouble your sleep. Some you will feel frustrated over because you can't influence it and some is simply frightening. We can swallow limitless quantities of news bits and pieces – most instantly forgotten. News often misleads and often focuses on the wrong things. Fake or inaccurate news misdirects.

Google CEO, Sundar Pichai, has written that his company should be held accountable for combating the spread of fake news, "I view it as a big responsibility to get it right. I think we'll be able to do these things better over time." Google has been criticized for failing to weed out fake news. It's not alone. Unfortunately, good news doesn't sell. We're driven by fear and conspiracy theories – two of the most powerful drivers – and people love it. The news outlets understand this and most of them exploit it. Social media fosters the fear and conspiracy theories and the circle is complete.

News dumbs us down – it does all the thinking for us. We don't come to our own conclusions. Sociologist Pierre Bordieu points out that, "News is a series of apparently absurd stories that all end up looking the same, endless parades of poverty-stricken countries, sequences of events that, having appeared with no explanation, will disappear with no solution – Zaire today, Bosnia yesterday, the Congo tomorrow." Harsh perhaps, but true.

We get anxious when we're cut off from the flow of news. We have to check our phones every 30 seconds. And news often has no explanatory power. Occurrences need rationale and either we're not offered that or terrible events can't be explained. And, worst of all, really worst of all and the bane of many lives, news feeds the mother of all cognitive errors: confirmation bias. In the words of Warren Buffett, "What the human being is best at doing is interpreting all new information so that their prior conclusions remain intact." That's frightening. News also exacerbates the story bias. Our brains crave stories that make sense – even if they don't correspond to reality. Then we make stuff up to fill the holes.

The repetition of news about things upon which we can't act makes us passive. It grinds us down until we adopt a worldview that is pessimistic. But, we do have control over how much news we take on-board and when. And, if turning away from the news, or some news, helps our growth and allows us some space, then that's a benefit.

The practice

- Thích Nhât Hanh, a Vietnamese Buddhist monk and peace activist, wrote, "When you turn on the television, for instance, you run the risk of ingesting harmful things, such as violence, despair or fear."

- Out of all the news stories you've read in the last twelve months, name one that allowed you to make a better decision about a serious matter affecting your life, your career or your business.

- The more news facts you digest, the less of the big picture you understand.

- When you take a break from breaking news you can sleep better, be more optimistic, laugh more freely and become less stressed. Try it.

- Take a regular digital rest. Once a day or for a full day every week, unplug. Disconnect everything so that you can fully connect to what matters most in your life.

- Leave your phone at home from time to time. Dare you!

- If you listen to news in your car, switch to music or silence.

GIVE YOURSELF CREDIT

Mindset change requires you to feel good about yourself. You know that much. This process is enhanced if we congratulate ourselves for doing things that we set out to achieve.

The idea

Leadership specialist Simon Sinek said in his TED Talk, *How Great Leaders Inspire Action*, that no one follows a leader for the leader. He said that they follow a leader for themselves. The most inspirational leaders ignite a spark within their employees (or their people) that move them to action. The spark gives them, the employees/the people, 'permission' to take credit.

We've all experienced instances in which credit was given unfairly and where others took credit for our work. Sometimes credit is assigned to the wrong individuals. We're taught that modesty is a noble trait – something we need to develop – and that vanity, arrogance and self-promotion are undesirable. Taking credit for what we've done well is fine. Taking credit is fine; being arrogant isn't.

In *Feeling Good: The New Mood Therapy*, David Burns lists the 'cognitive distortions' typical of depressed thinking, "Disqualifying the positive is one of the most destructive forms of cognitive distortion. You're like a scientist intent on finding evidence to support some pet hypothesis. The hypothesis that dominates your depressive thinking is usually some version of 'I'm second-rate.'" And it's often women who take little credit when credit is due. Writer, Kay Steiger, shares this: "For too many women, the hardest part of being successful might be taking credit for the work that they do, especially when they work in groups." Digital marketing expert Maggie Fox adds, "I don't care how distasteful you find it... Women who want to 'change the ratio', but don't self-promote are letting all of us down."

We don't take enough time to congratulate ourselves for our achievements. We sometimes pay little attention to our smaller accomplishments because we become so focused on our long-term goals. Often when we feel frustrated or upset, we only concentrate on the mistakes we've made. If you find yourself thinking you should have done this or that differently, then don't beat yourself up. Learn and give yourself credit for what you did do well. There will have been something.

The practice

- Allow yourself to feel confident about the things you've accomplished, even if you've messed up in other areas.

- If you congratulate yourself for a small task you completed, you start creating some positive momentum. This positive energy will keep you going through tougher times.

- If you don't appreciate yourself, who do you think should appreciate you?

- When you have positive thoughts about yourself, you behave positively.

ACCEPT THAT PROBLEMS ARE INEVITABLE BUT THEY CAN BECOME OPPORTUNITIES

OF COURSE, MOST OF us react negatively to problems when they take us by surprise. Problems are a given – only the intensity of the problems are a variable. If you can learn to accept problems as a normal, regular and completely unavoidable part of life, then you'll have taken your first step toward handling them with more positivity, grace and objective understanding. And problems *can* be opportunities.

The idea

"Stress primarily comes from not taking action over something that you can have some control over," Amazon's Jeff Bezos wrote. Problems in life are, like many things (including opportunities), inevitable. But fighting that inevitability is one of the biggest energy drains. Those who suffer daily with worry, anxiety and stress can find life turning into one long dark tunnel. It's therefore important to know where to focus our time and energy and where not.

We must problem-solve and doing that is refreshing. It's also how businesses grow. Great companies are those that dedicate themselves to a problem/opportunity that matters. Companies that survive do so because what they exist to solve or deliver is so big that there is still work to do. Purina, for example, exists to 'connect pets with people.' Google exists to 'organize the world's information.' When will missions like that be achieved? Each day – and never – which is why, as long of course as they stick to and achieve their objectives, they will survive.

When we learn from our mistakes (and we must), we should try and become the kind of person who welcomes obstacles and setbacks as opportunities. Those who say that problems are only ever opportunities are wrong, because they are by no means always that. Some difficulties in life are big and are hard or impossible to surmount. With most problems though, there are solutions and the solution-finding can be managed in a positive way. If we tackle anything in a negative mindset, then the results will never be satisfactory. It's also very easy to over-generalize when dealing with problems. Having an awful day might be defined by losing your favourite pen. That doesn't equal a bad day.

In 1941, annoyed with burs always getting attached to his socks and to his dog, Swiss engineer George de Mestral decided after a hike in the Alps to look at the burs under the microscope to find out why they stuck so well. He found the tiny hooks that allowed the burs to attach to the fabric of his socks and his dog's fur. This 'problem solving' led to the invention of Velcro. In 2010, the Deep Water Horizon rig exploded in the Gulf of Mexico, unleashing the largest single oil spill in history. This three-month uncontrolled release of crude oil from the sea floor (over a mile deep) created an unprecedented problem and an environmental disaster. No technology existed to contain it. BP's Capping Stack that ultimately brought the release under control was developed in two months out of necessity – and is now incorporated in deep water drilling operations across the globe. The Asian financial crisis of 1997/98 plunged affected countries into deep recessions, rapidly increasing unemployment and poverty. Although devastating for these countries, particularly Indonesia and Thailand, the crisis provided valuable lessons that would stand Asia in good stead for the global crisis a decade later. Many agree that, as a result, Asian economies are better than they were in 1997. Large scale crises that challenge multiple interests have a way of pulling together diverse partners – allies and rivals alike – to solve a problem and create an opportunity.

The practice

- Don't magnify problems. Yes, some are huge, but most aren't.

- From every experience there are always lessons to learn and this is where you can grow and improve.

- Sometimes problems aren't as big as you might think. Not having your suitcase on arrival at an airport is a nuisance, but it isn't the end of the world.

- Challenges often come from how we resist change. Don't resist change just because you *fear* change.

- If facing a problem means that you have to change your views on something and you feel instinctively that the new views are sound, then you'll know that your mindset is changing for the better.

REMEMBER, YOU ALWAYS HAVE CHOICES

In Lewis Carroll's *Alice in Wonderland*, Alice came to a fork in a road. "Which road do I take?" she asked. "Where do you want to go?" replied the Cheshire cat. "I don't know," Alice answered. "Then," said the cat, "it doesn't matter." How you interpret challenges, setbacks and criticisms is your choice. With a fixed mindset, you can interpret them in the belief that your talents are finite. With a growth mindset, you can stretch yourself, expand your abilities and manage choice. It's up to you.

The idea

Life is filled with choices and wouldn't be the same without them. Throughout our lives we often wonder whether or not we should turn left or right or should do this or that. The wonderful thing is that we do have a choice. The hardest thing is also the fact that we have a choice.

One of the decision-making mistakes we commonly make is to give ourselves options. We believe that, if we consider every possible alternative, we'll have better choices and make best decisions. We assume that if we go through every option, there will be no uncertainty. The problem is that we're likely to get overwhelmed and make no decision. And uncertainty will remain.

Martin Gilbert of Aberdeen Asset Management adds, "When we bought Deutsche Asset Management in 2005, it comes down to me in a room with the guy from Deutsche, so there is that loneliness at these crucial points. But up until then, we do discuss things hugely. We are largely consensus-driven. For me to go out and try and do something without taking my people with me would be suicidal." For Hong Kong-based entrepreneur Allan Zeman, of the Lan Kwai Fong Group, his take on choices is speed, "You've got to face problems and you've got to be able to react – and react very quickly."

In 1997 Apple chose to bring back Steve Jobs whom they'd fired. Sometimes boards are quick to jettison a founder in favour of professional management. But for all a company might gain from bringing in a pro, it risks losing magic and entrepreneurial vigour. In 1993, Tata Steel's CEO, J.J. Irani, made a choice that led to a novel approach to layoffs. It boosted employee morale while saving money. This was an antiquated and money losing Tata Steel plant in Jamshedpur, India. Some employees were going to lose their jobs. No one had ever lost a job at Tata Steel. Once you worked there, your job was guaranteed and after 25 years you were guaranteed that your son or daughter could work there too. So, the new deal was that workers under the age of 40 would be guaranteed their full salary for the rest of their working lives. Older workers would be guaranteed an amount greater than their salary, from 20 per cent to 50 per cent depending on their age. If they died before reaching retirement age, their families would keep receiving the full payments until the worker would have reached that age. By 2004, the workforce had shrunk from 78,000 to 47,000, with about a third of the reduction from natural attrition. Lower labour costs, combined with over $1 billion of new investment, turned Tata Steel into an efficient, globally competitive firm.

In 1952, Boeing relied on the 707. CEO Bill Allen decided to launch the plane, even though he had no orders. He simply believed customers would buy. It takes courage to wager a company's future on a vision. In 1982, when Johnson & Johnson learned that bottles of its Tylenol sold in Chicago had been laced with cyanide and seven people had died, CEO James Burke withdrew every bottle of the painkiller nationally and then designed a tamper-proof bottle – all at a cost of $100 million.

The decision-making process of 'on the one hand' and 'on the other' is tough. Some people enjoy this. Others are terrified of and by it. Some go into a decision knowing that the alternative was probably the better option and therefore they set themselves up to fail. The most frustrating, but equally most important thing about this is that we know there is an answer. We just have to decide.

The practice

- Listen to your instinct. You could try this: when faced with two choices, simply toss a coin... because in that brief moment when the coin is in the air, you might suddenly know what choice you wanted.

- The challenge of staying positive is tough while struggling to determine what choice is best. Life rarely presents black and white options. It's up to you to use your skills – and your support systems – to work out what's best.

- Nobody can deny the value of getting input from others. When it comes to making big life decisions, you may have to make them with others in mind, but sometimes it may be all up to you.

- Believe in the choices you've made.

- Once you've made your choice, make sure that you commit yourself to it and refuse to look back. Stay positive.

JUST SAY NO

WE HAVE A GLOBAL culture of over-commitment. Many people say 'yes' to things they don't really want to do and this feeds negativity. You don't always have to put the needs of others in front of your own – and you don't have to feel guilty about putting yours first.

The idea

Warren Buffett comments, "The difference between successful people and very successful people is that very successful people say 'no' to almost everything." Adam Grant, Wharton School professor, author of *Give and Take*, writes, "If you want something done, ask a busy person. The old saying rings true, but it also spells doom for that busy person... When you develop a reputation for being responsive and generous, an ever-expanding mountain of requests will come your way."

Saying 'no' in any scenario doesn't need to be an act of rejection. Learning to say no the right way can prove that we're receptive and able. Or that we're a soft touch. Successful people take the time to understand why each request is important to the person asking, as it shows they care even if they don't have time to help.

It's crucial to fully understand our own objectives before we can decide which requests to accept. Successful people take a goal first approach, in which they define their own major objectives and only agree to help with projects that work toward these goals. Selfish? Could be, but not really because it makes sense to have priorities – and we can't do everything. The key is to digest the information and its importance fast so we can get on to the next one. "Let me think about it" responses are unhelpful and invariably end up as a 'no' anyway. We are more respected for making decisions in a timely way, even if the choice is unwelcome. Of course, sometimes we want to help because we want to help.

Lucy Kellaway, writing in the *Financial Times* in 2017, noted that, "Despite being a great fan of 'no' at work, even I admit that sometimes it is the wrong answer. The great challenge is therefore to spot when to stop saying 'no' and start saying 'yes'... The main difference between 'yes' and 'no' is that one is easy and the other hard. 'Yes' can be said by any old fool, while 'no' requires character, commitment and courage... If you procrastinate, you are already on the back foot and may be tricked into saying 'yes' by mistake."

Former British prime minister Tony Blair said that, "The art of leadership is saying 'no', not saying 'yes'. It's very easy to say 'yes'." But, declining without an explanation makes our answers harsh because it doesn't allow the other person to understand reasoning. Explaining the 'why' makes the 'what' simple to digest, although we're not obliged to explain – and explaining can end up becoming an argument. There's a book called *How to Say No Without Feeling Guilty* by Patti Breitman where the premise is precisely that you can say 'no' without feeling guilt. And Steve Jobs is said to have commented, "It's only by saying 'no' that you can concentrate on the things that are really important."

The practice

- Say 'no' out of strength instead of 'yes' out of weakness.

- 'No' is an important word to use in time management as it can help allocate your time to things that are more important to you.

- Identify what's important to you and what's not. If you don't know where you want to spend your time, you won't know where you don't want to spend your time.

- Thank people for making a request. This doesn't need to lead to a 'yes'.

- Be straightforward with your 'no'. Do not say 'maybe' or 'possibly.' It comes across as unclear.

- Don't lie about your reasons for saying 'no'.

- Say 'no' to the request, not the person. You're not rejecting the person, just declining his/her invitation. Make that clear.

- Some people don't give up easily. That's their prerogative. But without violating any of the rules above, give yourself permission to be just as pushy as they are.

- Think about the anguish and resentment that saying 'yes' has caused you. Wouldn't it be so much easier and straightforward to just say 'no' in the first place?

CHAPTER 6
ATTITUDE TOWARDS OTHERS

SAY THANK YOU

MOST OF US TAKE a lot for granted. Thank those in your life who make it positive, better and happier.

The idea

Author and speaker Zig Ziglar wrote that, "gratitude is the healthiest of all human emotions. The more you express gratitude for what you have, the more likely you will have even more to express gratitude for." According to a Harvard Health publication, "Managers who remember to say 'thank you' to people who work for them may find that those employees feel motivated to work harder." When Frank Blake became CEO of The Home Depot in 2007, he established a process for writing notes: regional and district managers sent him recommendations of store associates whose work or service deserved recognition. Blake wrote them 'thank you' notes by hand – and was inspired by what he received back.

Good manners are a code of conduct or rules, based on common sense, courtesy and usage. Gratitude is one of these. Since we were children, most of us have known that some situations require thanks. There have always been ill-mannered people, but this doesn't mean that you are or want to be. It's important to say thank you because we recognize that someone had a choice – they didn't have to do something in a certain way whether it was opening a door or doing something more significant.

In 2014, the year of Facebook's 10th anniversary, Mark Zuckerberg revealed that he was challenging himself to write one thank-you note each day. Douglas Conant, the former Campbell's Soup CEO, says he wrote at least 30,000 thank-you notes to employees over the course of his 10-year career leading the business. General Electric CEO Jack Welch and George H.W. Bush were famous thank-you writers. For economist Adam Smith, gratitude – the feeling of reverence for what others give to us – is the glue to healthy communities: "The duties of gratitude are perhaps the most sacred of those which the beneficent virtues prescribe to us." Empirical science agrees: gratitude, even a simple 'thank you', is a basis of power.

Saying thank you acknowledges respect. We should appreciate the act of a good deed and the time it took to perform that deed. It's important because we are a time-deprived society. People will, by and large, offer more help after being thanked because they feel better or because it boosts their own self-esteem. Mostly, it's because they appreciate being needed and feel more socially valued when they've been thanked. Gratitude is all about worth. Yours. And if you feel better because you've been thanked or because you've thanked someone, well that's going to boost your positivity.

Gratitude is a great motivational tool and, anyway, who doesn't like to be thanked? What is surprising is how hard it is to do the thanking. 'Cheers' won't do.

The practice
- Try sending a handwritten thank you note.

- Everyone craves appreciation. As social creatures, we are motivated by acceptance.

- The key to leadership, in Dale Carnegie's book *How to Win Friends and Influence People* is to be, "hearty in your approbation and lavish in your praise."

- Gratitude increases people's self-esteem, which is an essential component to optimal performance and growth mindset.

DON'T PLACE YOUR FUTURE IN SOMEONE ELSE'S HANDS

WE ALL HAVE A boss of some kind and even the highest in the land have stakeholders to whom they must answer. We're all accountable to somebody. And we all need other people. But, be that as it may, your future is predominantly yours alone to shape.

The idea

Act like the new leader, manager, employee from day one. In shouldering responsibility, we are giving ourselves the power to shape the outcome of any action ourselves and are therefore taking an active and not a passive role in how the outcome turns out. It's only when we accept that everything we are or ever will be is up to us, that we're able to get rid of the negativity of excuse-making that can so often prevent success.

Industrialist, Andrew Carnegie, didn't build a huge fortune because of professional experience or formal education. He dropped out of school and worked in a cotton mill, as a messenger and then in the railroad industry. He taught himself by reading. Debbi Fields was just over twenty years old when she started Mrs. Fields Cookies. She had no training in the food industry. She used earnings from working as a ball girl at Oakland Athletics games to buy ingredients for her cookies.

The more personal responsibility we take, the more in control we are and the more control we have. Then we will more likely reach our goal as there will be no excuses to fall back on if we do fail. As business author Jim Rohn writes, "You must take personal responsibility. You cannot change the circumstances, the seasons or the wind, but you can change yourself. That is something you have charge of."

The founder of Mary Kay Cosmetics did have some work experience, but no formal education or entrepreneurial training, before starting her company in 1963. It was after being passed over for a promotion in favour of a man (she had trained), that she wrote a book aimed at helping women succeed in business which became the business plan that she used to launch Mary Kay Cosmetics. Joyce Hall, the founder of Hallmark Cards, started his career with no real experience in the product that would later make his family name the brand for cards. His first venture was selling perfume to neighbours after which he got a job as a clerk. At 16, he opened the Norfolk Postcard Company in Nebraska. Circumstances forced him to produce his own cards only when a fire destroyed his existing stock. Coco Chanel learned to sew not via formal training, but from making and altering her own clothes while living in a convent orphanage. Later she made hats as a hobby and sold them to other boutiques before opening up on her own.

All of these people and many others started their successful careers by relying mostly on themselves. Once we accept responsibility for (mostly) everything that happens to us in life, we'll discover that this also enables us to find solutions to life's difficulties. "Hold yourself responsible for a higher standard than anybody expects of you. Never excuse yourself," wrote preacher, Henry Ward Beecher. Most of us will have come across descriptions of successful people where words such as 'persistence', 'perseverance' and 'tenacity' have been used to describe them. They put their futures in their own hands. That doesn't mean that we can't take advice from others but, when all the information has been gathered, the responsibility is ours.

Some people give up at the first sign of difficulty. The reason to stop may of course be valid (wrong job, wrong boss, insufficient skills), but we're so aware of the desperate need not to be seen to stumble that we often stop at the first sign of a bump in the road. Or, we blame the decision on the fact that we think we 'can't'. Much of this will stem from listening to what others have to say that isn't helpful and people saying that we 'should' or that we 'mustn't' or 'if I were you'. It's important to sort out the wheat from the chaff, the good support from the negative.

The practice

- Don't give anyone too much influence.

- Be everything you want to be. You have more potential than anyone you know.

- Whatever decisions you make, make them your own.

- Friends, family and colleagues will listen to your problems and some will try and push you, but they can't be responsible for your achievements – or failures.

- You can't control what other people say and do, but you can decide for yourself what you're going to do.

53 YOU'RE NOT ALONE

HAVING JUST SAID THAT we must rely on ourselves, successful people also recognize other people's contributions to their success. While what we do we do ourselves, most of us need and get support without which or whom we probably wouldn't make it.

The idea
John Donne wrote:
"No man is an island,
Entire of itself;
Every man is a piece of the continent,
A part of the main."

In life, there are obviously different types of people we all need. They help us in our endeavours. As mythologist Joseph Campbell points out in *The Hero's Journey*, all great heroes have a mentor. Luke Skywalker had Yoda. Steve Jobs served as a mentor to Mark Zuckerberg. Christian Dior mentored Yves St Laurent. Woody Guthrie mentored Bob Dylan. The Karate Kid had Mr. Miyagi. Bill Gates had Warren Buffet. If you follow the *Hunger Games* books and movies, you'll know that Katniss Everdeen had Haymitch Abernathy. A mentor is someone who has huge amounts of experience, is a great listener and someone who likes you and your ambitions. S/he is someone to whom you can turn.

If we want to grow our business, we can align ourselves with someone who has succeeded with a similar business model. If we want to lose weight, we can get a personal trainer or we could reach out to a friend who has already succeeded in his or her weight loss. Batman is better with Robin. Neo needed Trinity. Buzz Lightyear and Woody. Butch

Cassidy and The Sundance Kid. Bob Hope and Bing Crosby. Holmes and Watson. Lennon and McCartney. Ben and Jerry. Wallace and Gromit. The point is, we all need someone to cheer us on. Not someone who's responsible for our success, but someone who can help enable it.

We are not alone in feeling alone sometimes. So, no matter how embarrassed or pathetic we feel about our own situation, we must know that there are others experiencing the same emotions. Sometimes when you're lonely, you *need* to be alone – not to be lonely, but to enjoy some free time just being yourself and finding your way. That's part of growth too.

The practice

- Being alone does not mean that you're lonely and being lonely doesn't mean you're alone.

- Call or meet someone who's trustworthy, always supportive or who simply makes you laugh.

- Help someone in need. Helping others makes us less self-focused.

- Like an unwelcomed visitor, loneliness will leave.

- While accountability for your success is yours, there's no shame in discussing ideas with a trusted partner, friend or colleague.

54 VISUALIZE A SUCCESSFUL OUTCOME

VISUALIZATION TECHNIQUES ARE USED by successful people to see what their desired outcomes will look like. 'Will' is an important word.

The idea

"Everything you can imagine is real," said Pablo Picasso and that's a tough one to prove. But, Michael Jordan always took the last shot in his mind before he ever took one in real life. Boxing legend Muhammad Ali was always stressing the importance of seeing himself victorious before the fight. Anything of note will have been visualized – flight, telephones, steam trains, space travel, the four-minute mile, the atomic bomb. By being able to paint a concrete picture of what success looks like to us, it becomes less abstract and more achievable. When we know what we're looking for, we're programmed to be receptive to opportunities that are aligned to our targets.

Harvard marketing guru Ted Levitt believed that, "The future belongs to people who see possibilities before they become obvious." The daily practice of visualizing our objectives as if they already existed can rapidly accelerate our achievement of any (achievable) ambition. The process activates our creativity, imagination and then ideas. If we can see what an end result looks like, it makes it easier to achieve. Visualization programmes the brain to perceive and recognize the resources and stages needed to achieve a specific objective. And, like anything to do with mindset change, being specific is as important as being positive.

Athletes call the end-result visualization process 'mental rehearsal'. But obviously they and we have to imagine within scope; if we can't run fast then we're unlikely to be a Usain Bolt. And talking of Usain Bolt, he visualized the outcome of most of his races. The best footballers visualize the ball in the back of the net, golfers the ball in the hole.

Visualization works because neurons in our brains interpret imagery as the equivalent of real action. When we visualize an act, the brain generates an impulse that tells our neurons to perform the movement. This creates a new neural pathway – brain cells that work together to create learned behaviour that primes us in a way consistent with what we imagined. Oh yes, apparently, years after Disneyland and Disney World were completed, someone said to Mike Vance, the then Creative Director of Walt Disney Studios, "Isn't it a shame that Walt Disney didn't live long enough to see this?" Apparently, Mike Vance replied, "But he did see it. That's why it's here."

The practice

- Imagine the process, not just the end-result.

- If your challenge is more mental than physical – for instance, handling a difficult conversation or a tough meeting – imagining the outcome you'd like can keep you calm and focused.

- Create a detailed vision of what you want to achieve. See, hear and feel what you want to happen in all its detail.

- Take people with you. Many people have a goal and target it and sometimes they get what they want but, in the process, alienate people around them.

DON'T ACCEPT NEGATIVITY FROM OTHER PEOPLE

WHY? WELL, ANY NEGATIVITY in others can bring you down to their level and that doesn't help you at all. Again, positive or negative options rear their heads and you have to choose positive.

The idea

Ellen Pao, former interim CEO of the online community Reddit, stepped down after facing a torrent of abuse. Pao's troubles began after the site shut down five forums considered to be racist. Anonymous users flooded the website with ugly commentary and the result was a petition against Pao. Despite the complaints lodged against her, Pao conducted herself professionally, refusing to answer the negativity in kind.

There's no shortage of pessimists. There'll always be people who can find the negative in life, people who share their problems and fail to seek (or accept) solutions. They want us to join their dark view so they can feel better – and we may feel pressured to listen and get sucked in to their world. It's difficult but the only way to manage this is to excuse ourselves or to inject positive topics with which we know the other person has empathy. Maintaining a level of emotional detachment is vital for keeping stress at a distance.

Not allowing negative people to put their inadequacies onto you is key to your emotional and mindset health. David J. Pollay, author of *The Law of the Garbage Truck* believes that, "Many people are like garbage trucks. They run around full of garbage, full of frustration, full of anger and full of disappointment. As their garbage piles up, they look for a place to dump it. And if you let them, they'll dump it on you...

Don't take it personally. Just smile, wave, wish them well, and move on... You'll be happier."

The practice

- Negative people should get the least of your time and energy, yet we often give them the most attention.

- Don't be taken in by the angry people and try to control what is out of your control i.e. other people's behaviour. You can't.

- If distancing yourself from negative people is impossible, you can set limits by asking a negative person how s/he intends to manage the problem about which she is complaining.

- Consider whether you understand a negative person's situation and think through whether you can offer options that will help this person. But don't spend masses of time on this. For the most part, you can't change people and you shouldn't try.

56

SEE THINGS FROM SOMEBODY ELSE'S POINT OF VIEW

'BEFORE YOU CRITICIZE A man, walk a mile in his shoes' is a well-known proverb. We can (if we try) change our patterns of thought by trying to see things from another point of view, whether it's that of colleagues, bosses, partners, parents or just someone impartial. This can help you see where you might have gone wrong or why others might be right. It can help us to understand something important and, once again, help us to be more positive.

The idea

In *To Kill a Mockingbird*, Harper Lee wrote, "You never really know a man until you understand things from his point of view, until you climb into his skin and walk around in it." It's beneficial to see things from the perspective of the people with whom we live or work. We become aware of not only our own actions, but the *consequences* of those actions. One example of this in action is Facebook's *Empathy Lab*, which gives Facebook engineers the chance to experience for themselves how customers will use their products – even if those customers are visually impaired or hard of hearing. The hope is that designers will understand what their customers are experiencing and build products that take their needs into account. Empathy at work.

Henry Ford wrote, "If there is any one secret of success, it lies in the ability to get the other person's point of view and see things from that person's angle as well as from your own." And Indra Nooyi (PepsiCo's CEO) comments on staff interaction, "I'm very honest – brutally honest. I always look at things from their point of view as well as mine. And I know when to walk away." If we can see things differently, from another person's perspective, we can have fewer disagreements and more constructive responses to contentious issues. We'll be careful about what we say or do in a difficult situation and avoid escalating the negatives.

By taking another person's point of view, we broaden our own. Empathy is important. U.S. product designer Patricia Moore's specialty was using empathy to cross the generational gulf. Her best-known experiment was in the late 1970s when, aged 26, she dressed as an 85-year-old woman to see what life was like as an older person. She put on ageing makeup, wore fogged-up glasses, wrapped her hands with bandages to simulate arthritis and wore uneven shoes so that she hobbled. She visited cities dressed like this, trying to do ordinary things but from an old person's point of view. Based on her experiences, she invented new products easily used by older people.

The practice

- Work on your ability to see how a specific situation or issue might seem to others.

- When you see others' points of view, it allows you to be more empathetic – even if you don't agree with their point of view.

- Empathy means awareness and understanding, knowing where another person is coming from and that other person 'getting' where *you're* coming from too.

- A limitation we face is that we look at the world from our own subjective perspective. We can't help it. Where there's something personal at stake, we have a built-in bias (based on beliefs which can change as you know).

57 DON'T LOOK BACK IN ANGER

People get angry in arguments fuelled by blame. They want to prove they're right – and often insist. This is a waste of time and energy. Though it might be fun for the ego to go around saying, "He was wrong and bad and I'm right and good," nothing of value is accomplished. Instead of blaming others, work out what happened and learn. And move on.

The idea

There are many examples of successful high profilers who are famous for tirades – Gordon Ramsay, Rahm Emanuel, Meg Whitman, Donald Trump. People get frustrated and angry. Elizabeth Holmes founded Theranos' new blood-testing technology in 2003, but, undoubtedly frustrated, held back information on its equipment when it faced scrutiny in 2015. Her mismanagement damaged the company's reputation and U.S. federal regulators banned Holmes from the lab-testing business for two years.

Musk's reactions to a Tesla driver's death have been well documented. Experts refer to his angry, defensive response and use of statistics to suggest the death was not as significant as it should have been to him. Martin Shkreli, founder and former CEO of Turing Pharmaceuticals, raised the price of an AIDS and cancer drug to $750 a pill to improve profits and was separately charged with defrauding investors. A convicted felon, he ruined a reputation, not just because of his actions, but based on his arrogant antics in court and social media. All three violated the basic principles of crisis management: accept responsibility, apologize, make amends and changes to ensure it never happens again.

Uber's former CEO Travis Kalanick had a short fuse. Many people have issues with anger, not all of them in the spotlight. Yelling at one of his drivers was bad behaviour that displayed a lack of Kalanick's leadership skills. Anger is an emotion and too many people have too little control over their emotions. Conversely, in 2016, Whole Foods was accused of grossly overcharging customers for certain items. Overcoming some initial missteps, joint CEOs Walter Robb and John Mackey delivered a video message to accept responsibility. "Straight up, we made some mistakes. We want to own that and tell you what we're doing about it," Robb said. Any anger on any side was dissipated. René Redzepi was chef for fifteen years at Copenhagen's Noma, the restaurant consistently ranked as one of the world's best. He succeeded, at least initially, by shouting. But then he changed and has called for an end to chefs' use of "bullying and humiliation in order to wring results out of their cooks".

A fixed-mindset doesn't easily allow anyone to change course. Blame is a big part of the fixed-mindset; when something goes wrong people don't want to take responsibility because that would be accepting inferiority. Blame very often equals anger that is never managed. This can push some to become abusive and controlling. They feel superior by making others feel inferior. Anger solves little and creates negativity.

In any anger relating to what we think someone has done to us, we need to look back at what the person actually *did* do. Does it still seem as important now as it did when it first happened? If not, then we might want to try forgiving the person for his/her/their action. If what they did seems unforgivable, though, then we need to move on. Energy spent on old hurts won't help us. Forgiveness benefits the forgiver, not just the forgiven. So, when someone says, "I can forgive, but never forget," don't believe them. Let it go.

The practice
- Anger can show you care. It's a sign that something has moved you. (As opposed to *rage*, which is the usually negative response to often misplaced anger).

- Anger can ignite action. But, mostly it ignites reaction and that's not usually positive.

- Anger can cloud our judgment and we can become consumed with pain; we make irrational, unreasonable, regretful and hurtful decisions.

- Anger tends to lock us into a single way of thinking about what happened. That interpretation becomes a sore that won't heal. So, the aim is to forget – or not let the issue cause you pain.

- Often, when you're angry with somebody, you tend to think repeatedly about the thing they did to you, which keeps you emotionally engaged. Don't ruminate. Move on.

GET YOUR ATTITUDE RIGHT

YOUR ATTITUDE PLAYS A big part in your life and can affect how the future works out for you. If we have a negative attitude, always expecting the worst and never enjoying what we already have, we'll find that our choices are limited. Your attitude rubs off on your colleagues, family and friends. If you maintain a positive one, it'll be infectious and those around you will pick up on your energy.

The idea

Attitude is defined as a manner, disposition, feeling or position with regard to a person or thing. It's the 'face' that you choose to have. John Maxwell, in his book, *Developing the Leaders around You*, writes, "A positive attitude is one of the most valuable assets a person can have in life." Organizational theorist, Robert Anthony, affirms, "Forget about all the reasons why something may not work. You only need to find one good reason why it will." Attitude is of course part of our mindsets and covers the breadth of our view of the world and how we manage it.

Tom Davin was CEO at Taco Bell and Panda Express. He said, "The only control we have in life is our positive mental attitude." Positivity breeds positivity. As our mindset develops, our values, beliefs and opinions become clearer and will have changed from what they were. Similarly, we will want to do and think things that support what we've become. When we take action, we must always take steps to act with a purpose, so that our actions are in tandem with our values. Businesses do or did this with their single-minded propositions. From Fedex ('When your package absolutely, positively has to get there overnight') to Coca-Cola ('It's the real thing') to 'Avis is only number 2. So we try harder.' William James, an early 20th century philosopher, wrote, "It is our attitude at the beginning of a difficult undertaking which, more than anything else, will determine its successful outcome."

When Harland Sanders reached the age of 65, after running a restaurant for several years, he found himself penniless. He travelled to houses and restaurants all over his local area. He wanted to partner with someone to promote his chicken recipe. He had little luck. He started to cook his fried chicken on the spot for restaurant owners. If the owner liked the result, they would agree to sell the Colonel's chicken – for every piece of chicken the restaurant sold, Sanders would get a nickel. The restaurant would receive packets of the Colonel's herbs and spices. It is said that before he heard his first 'yes please', he heard a thousand 'no thanks'. By 1964, Colonel Sanders had 600 franchises selling his chicken. He sold his company for $2 million dollars in 1964 and remained the company's brand.

The practice

- Smile more – and mean it.

- Proactivity, like positivity, will help with your mindset development. A reactive person allows others and external events to determine how s/he will feel. A proactive person decides how s/he will feel *regardless* of what may be going on around them.

- Try not to complain for seven days and instead replace any negative thought with a positive one. Expect the very best out of every situation.

- Don't compare yourself to others. Don't ever say "it's not fair."

- Sarcasm can be fun but, in the end, it's just negativity wrapped up and packaged as a joke. And it can hurt. Drop the sarcasm – you don't need to ridicule things you don't like.

BE INSPIRED

WE ARE INSPIRED BY others – people whom we admire for their achievements. We admire courageous people, actors, musicians, leaders, achievers in sports, business, politics, social responsibility. We need role models and good ones to help us grow – and from whom we can learn.

The idea

We all have inspirational models whether it's the likes of Anne Frank, Shakespeare, Leonardo da Vinci, Lionel Messi – and we all have favourites and for different reasons. Some inspirational people are below the radar and unsung – including the old lady across the road because she saved people's lives during a war/famine/disaster or a single mum or dad who's had to bring up three children alone.

Below the radar one might include the likes of Michael Ellott who worked tirelessly as the President of ONE, a global campaigning and advocacy organization taking action to end extreme poverty and preventable disease, particularly in Africa. Or Andrea Tamburini who worked tirelessly for Action Against Hunger as CEO in 2014. Above the parapet are the likes of David Karp of blogging platform Tumblr, valued at $800 million. Karp launched Tumblr when he was only 20, and the service took off within a matter of weeks. Now he has a net worth of more than $200 million. There were other blogging platforms when Tumblr was started. Karp recognized the need for a different format to appeal to those who wanted a short-form blogging platform but who were too limited by Twitter. Then there's Jared Hecht who at 23 helped found GroupMe, a group text-messaging service and sold it to Skype one year later for about $80 million. Not bad for one year of work as a CEO! The inspiration here is that if you have a good idea, you can develop it and sell it to someone else who can turn it into something more.

It's always inspiring to read about a CEO who started at the bottom. Ursula Burns did that at Xerox. Mary Barra started at GM in her student days and became CEO in 2013. Dennis Muilenberg joined Boeing as an engineering intern in 1985 and became president, chairman and chief executive officer in 2015. David Abney, who began as a package loader for UPS at age 19 became CEO in 2014.

Starbucks' Howard Schultz invested time and effort to improve communities in terms of education, race relations and fair trade. Bill Gates has offered philanthropy to the world's poorest and weakest. Dan Houser is a co-founder of the entertainment company Rockstar Games. Heard of Grand Theft Auto? Enough said – and that and he are inspirational to millions. Mukesh Ambani is chairman of India's Reliance Industries generating $61 billion in annual sales. Ambani has a personal fortune of over $23 billion and has inspired people by predicting that India will grow to become a $30 trillion economy by 2030. Robin Li is chairman of Baidu, China's Google equivalent. As with Google, Baidu constantly invests in the future and has partnered with Daimler, the maker of Chinese Mercedes-Benz, to provide software for their cars that allows drivers to access content from their smartphones and with BMW, he's building a self-driving car. All inspirational.

So, 'inspiring' comes in all shapes and is applied to label things that have the surface characteristics of *being* inspiring. Amazing stories about amazing people have the *potential* to be inspiring. As long as we can call somebody else's story inspiring, we don't have to become the CEO of a Fortune 500 company or compete in the Olympics or learn to play guitar like Dave Gilmour. We get the quick fix of feeling positive because we admire qualities in someone else – not always because we wish we could do what they do, but because we understand why the qualities they have are beneficial.

The key to inspiration within a mindset context is that of using *inspiration* to improve something in us. If we don't balance the inspiring achievements of others with some hard work to achieve our own personal goals, then that positive feeling we get is admiration only. Think why some people are inspirational (actually for good or bad). They will have forged their own path and demanded a tremendous show of strength, commitment, courage and perseverance. If for good, they are the embodiment of fortitude in the face of opposition, criticism, judgment and maybe unbeatable odds. If for bad, then that's another story isn't it?

The practice

- If someone says, "I have your back," they should mean it, without fail. That's inspirational. Whatever *you* say, you have to mean it too.

- When you ask inspirational people what motivates them, they talk about making other people or a wider group successful. They will often talk about 'we' not 'I'.

- People who inspire are deeply grateful. Uninspiring people are self-satisfied. They secretly believe their success is a natural result of being better than everyone else.

- People who inspire treasure their beliefs. And care about people.

UNDERSTAND DIVERSITY

WHILE SOME BELIEFS AND values may change, they should (must) remain your own. So, consider whether your opinions are indeed yours. Understanding your own cultural makeup is the first step to understanding the fact that others hold different values and beliefs and, hopefully, you can believe in or accept them as much as you do yours.

The idea

We're living in a world of growing division and tension and it's having an impact. Immigration is a recurrent theme, particularly in times of economic downturn (and big political platforms). Today the likelihood is that we're all going to work with people from various cultures, religions and backgrounds. Part of our development within today's societies must necessitate an open mind. With media as instant as it is and with conflicts reported as frequently as they are, it's easy to become biased. And shocked: Myanmar's alleged military action against the minority Muslim Rohingya population, the Armenian massacres by the Turks in 1915–16, the Nazi Holocaust, the expulsion of Germans from Polish and Czech territories after World War II, the Bangladesh War of Independence of 1971, the genocide killing in Pakistan of possibly millions, 500,000 Serbs expelled from Croatia and Bosnia in the 1990's and many murdered, Iraq's gassing of Kurds and so on ad nauseam – global and consistent.

Understanding diversity works. Sodexo employs over 400,000 globally. Over 40 per cent are women; 43 per cent of the board are female. Sodexo has found that employee engagement has increased as have gross profit and brand image. Tim Ryan, U.S. chairman of PWC has been working to create the largest CEO-driven business commitment to advance diversity and inclusion in America and beyond. The initiative, *CEO Action for Diversity and Inclusion* brings together 150 CEOs of the world's leading companies, representing over forty-five industries.

Kaiser Permanente is a global healthcare business with around 180,000 staff. As the largest managed care organization in the USA, the Kaiser Permanente labour force reflects no racial majority, with 60 per cent comprising of people of colour. Additionally, 75 per cent of all employees, 50 per cent of the executive team and 30 per cent of their physicians are women. Here's another: Novartis has 170,000 employees worldwide and believes that diversity is integral to success, because it then helps staff understand the unique needs of patients. Within the organization, the word 'disability' has been replaced with 'diverseability' because they don't view people living with disabilities as having a lack of ability, but rather having diverse skills and proficiencies.

Deutsche Bank has frequently been named as one of the top employers for women. The bank also helps women progress to senior positions and supports ethnic understanding. Another example: Marriott President Arne Sorenson published a letter on LinkedIn urging Donald Trump to use his position to promote inclusiveness: "...Everyone, no matter their sexual orientation or identity, gender, race, religion, disability or ethnicity should have an equal opportunity to get a job, start a business or be served by a business. Use your leadership to minimize divisiveness around these areas by letting people live their lives and by ensuring that they are treated equally in the public square."

The increasingly diverse global workforce has made cultural integration an imperative to garner exchange and understanding. It doesn't always work and it doesn't happen easily.

The practice
- Most studies surrounding diversity in the workplace have found that for every 1 per cent increase in gender diversity, company revenue increases by 3 per cent.

- Learn what you can about members of another culture.

- Accept your own naïveté. Cultural responsiveness may require you to forgive your own mistakes and certainly your ignorance.

- Avoid all stereotypes whether negative or positive. Stereotypes are unreliable. And unsafe.

- Being aware of positive differences between you and anyone else is an important trait in developing a strong, growth mindset. You don't have to like everyone but, unless there's something very wrong, you can respect most people and find out what they value and why.

CHAPTER 7
MINDSET AT WORK

61 | FACE UP TO CHANGE

CHANGE AT WORK (or at home) usually pushes us out of our comfort zone and that, in turn, makes it hard to accept a particular change. Sometimes the change is huge – job loss, new job, company merger, office move, new processes, new boss, dreadful boss, new rules, new colleagues, new home circumstances – and it can be hard to accept that change. It's easy to become negative. But change can be refreshing.

The idea

Irish political theorist, Edmund Burke wrote: "We must all obey the great law of change. It's the most powerful law of nature." Change usually results in some kind of upheaval in our lives. Someone will say "I didn't see that coming" – like a divorce, or getting fired, for example. Victim status usually follows. But the positive or negative spin usually evolves from the personal perspective we put on it. John F. Kennedy wrote: "Change is the law of life and those who look only to the past or present are sure to miss the future."

Most of us accept that the world is on a course of individual and collective improvement – even though there may be (deep) dips into brutality, dishonesty and catastrophes. Living conditions the world over improve every day, more people are educated, fewer live in poverty, there are more cures for diseases. Longevity is increasing and that itself shows a consolidation of progress. Entrepreneur Jim Rohm wrote that "Life does not get better by chance. It gets better by change."

Most people dislike change. Sometimes change is so uncomfortable that we are reluctant adapters – changing, but slowly – and possibly not properly – or unwillingly and therefore not positively. But (as you know) change is a constant – and can be a catalyst for making life better. 18th century French philosopher, Denis Diderot wrote, "There are things I can't force. I must adjust. There are times when the greatest change needed is a change of my viewpoint." And adds Swiss psychiatrist Carl Jung, "We cannot change anything unless we accept it."

Change occurs in our lives at regular intervals, whether we're aware of it or not. For a start, we all change. Yes, we do. Or a favourite shop that has been in your area for years may close down or an old building may be demolished to make way for a new road. You may lose something (or someone), there may be a divorce, the birth of a child, a longer commute – life isn't static, nor are *we* meant to be static either.

In 2014, Satya Nadella, as Microsoft's CEO, undertook a major restructuring to do away with damaging internal competition. Products and platforms would no longer exist as separate groups, but rather all employees would begin focusing on a set of common objectives. In 2016, Nadella shook things up again with the merging of the Microsoft Research Group with the Bing, Cortana, and Information Platform Group teams to create a new AI and Research Group. Nadella shared with employees a new sense of mission: "To empower every person and every organization on the planet to achieve more." He wrote, "Over the past year, we've challenged ourselves to think about our core mission, our soul – what would be lost if we disappeared..."

British Airways was created in 1974. The oil crises of the 1970s diminished the airline's customer base and its huge staff resulting in massive financial losses. The company developed a reputation for terrible service. In 1981, chairman Lord King restructured the organization by reducing its workforce from 60,000 to 40,000, eliminating unprofitable routes and modernizing the fleet. Not easy. He repaired the airline's image and within ten years, the airline reported the highest profits in its industry.

The practice

- See change as an adventure.

- Change creates movement that can lead to new opportunities. Newton's first law informs us that a moving object is likely to keep moving; an object at rest will stay at rest unless acted upon.

- We would often rather be unfulfilled and not quite happy in a situation we understand than trying a new, unknown path that provides the potential to find satisfaction. We must never settle for something solely because it's a known quantity.

- Think of a couple of big changes that have happened in your life. Did you resist the change when it first happened? Did anything positive result from the change?

- To accept change, you're going to have to let go of any fear of the unknown.

BE RESILIENT

In life, you can either let a challenge break you down and make you see the world in a negative light – or you can rise above it. Choose the latter. Sometimes the best way to deal with negative things in our lives is to take them head on. To consider resilience in business is to acknowledge that things are not always going to go well.

The idea

Resilience refers to any individual life experiences that might help us cope with adverse situations in a positive way by helping us deal with stress. Those who are resilient are able to cope better with anything that life throws their way. They believe in themselves and their ability to effectively manage challenges. Resilient people have a positive outlook. They know that what they're facing is mostly temporary – and that they've overcome setbacks before and can do so again. Before starting the Woolworth Company (now Foot Locker), Frank Woolworth worked at a dry goods store. His boss didn't allow him to be front of house because Woolworth, "didn't have enough common sense to serve the customers." The Woolworth Company was one of the original five-and-ten-cent stores, which is the model Sam Walton used to start Walmart.

Our world has become more and more out of balance. That's because of all sorts of things – terrorism (and the fear it generates), financial stress, pressure at work and home, dissatisfaction, ill health – overall all that life throws at us. It's sometimes hard to be resilient in responding to events. But resilience is an absolute necessity for growth.

Often, we tend to be reactive rather than preventative or proactive. We may only begin taking care of ourselves when we're confronted with a diagnosis or when a 'big thing' impinges on us. However, when 'big things' in our lives are properly understood, then there's a context for learning and growth. In business, management must take resilience seriously. Nurturing the right culture is key. This requires leadership from the top down and a relationship based on trust with staff, suppliers and other key stakeholders. At Virgin Atlantic, senior executives work in one corner of an open-plan office. Colleagues can come to them with their thoughts and there is a no-blame culture. As a result, vital risk information travels around the company and the board make well-informed decisions.

To find out what makes a company resilient, in 2016 researchers from the UK's Cranfield School of Management interviewed staff with risk management responsibilities at AIG, Drax, InterContinental Hotels, Jaguar Land Rover, The Technology Partnership, Virgin Atlantic and Zurich Insurance. It was clear that resilient companies don't just happen. They have cultural and behavioural traits that encourage all employees to be flexible, customer focused and alert to danger. They have the ability to anticipate problems before they develop and they prevent 'risk blindness'. They ensured that any one incident didn't escalate into a crisis and they learned from experience.

We've talked about visualization before and imagining what our world would be like after a change has taken place. Well, the same applies with resilience. Once faced with a difficulty, we often only picture a bad end result. 'Seeing' it in full allows us to plan accordingly. This is optimism. Optimism is the single biggest factor in recovering from adversity. It's what makes some of us seek out solutions to our troubles instead of hiding. We must *expect* that good things will happen.

Resilient people don't tend to make the same mistake again and again. They're willing to be honest about why they (or something in which they were involved) failed and they think about what didn't work. And then how to fix it for next time.

The practice

- Again (and no apologies) resilient people have a positive outlook. The tougher the situation, the tougher they become.

- Laughter dampens down our natural fight-or-flight reaction to minor negative events. It also shifts our perception of a difficult situation so that we can calm down, look at it from different angles and cope better.

- Life is what it is and doesn't necessarily get easier or more forgiving; but we can get stronger and more resilient in dealing with it.

- View decisions as active choices, not sacrifices. This helps maintain a high sense of control over the situation.

- Use the support available to you. And offer the same to others.

63 TAKE SHORT BREAKS

PEOPLE WHO ARE GIVEN (or who take) short breaks at work perform better than those who do without. Taking a short break in the middle of a long task re-energizes the brain. And keeps us positive.

The idea

Churchill, John F. Kennedy and Thomas Edison took regular rests each day. Churchill wrote, "Nature has not intended mankind to work from eight in the morning until midnight without that refreshment of blessed oblivion which, even if it only lasts twenty minutes, is sufficient to renew all the vital forces." Arianna Huffington adds, "Sleep makes us more productive, creative, less stressed and much healthier and happier... I grew up thinking that if you work around the clock, you are going to be more effective and I realise that is not true."

"When demand in our lives intensifies, we tend to hunker down and push harder," points out Tony Schwartz, head of New York City-based consulting firm The Energy Project which helps companies like Google, Apple, Facebook, Coca-Cola, Green Mountain Coffee and Ford to help them find better ways to work. "Without any downtime to refresh and recharge, we're less efficient, make more mistakes, and get less engaged with what we're doing."

We have a limited capacity for concentrating in one go and we may not recognize the symptoms of fatigue or distraction. Or boredom. No matter how engaged we are in an activity, our brains get tired. Short breaks replenish energy and improve focus. They enhance positivity and a 'can do' approach.

The practice

- Your maximum concentration on one thing in one go is around thirty minutes.

- Taking a break allows us to come back to the job at hand with renewed energy and sense of purpose.

- If you know you typically have an afternoon energy slump, consider a short lunchtime workout.

- Taking a break enables you to think and that can help address the topic on which you've been concentrating.

- If you don't schedule breaks into your calendar, you'll always feel that there's no time to take breaks.

- You need to take time away from all screens, notifications, beeps and messages.

- Productive is better than busy.

START YOUR DAY STRONG

64

SOME PEOPLE HAVE TO drag themselves out of bed and this sets a negative frame for their entire day. Positive people create a morning ritual that reinforces how great life is and how happy they are to be alive. Mindset growth needs positivity and positivity needs energy.

The idea

Mark Twain's line: "Eat a live frog first thing in the morning and nothing worse will happen to you for the rest of the day" basically means that we should start with the most difficult work item first thing – and then the rest of the day will seem easy. It's said that Mark Zuckerberg has only one type and colour of t-shirt so that making morning decisions can be avoided. John Paul DeJoria, the co-founder of Patrón tequila and Paul Mitchell hair products, starts every morning with five minutes of quiet reflection: "The very second I wake up, I stay in bed for about five minutes and just be."

Whatever's on our agenda, the day's going to happen regardless of our mindset. So, we should set our mindset to positive and move into the day from a good place. An inspiring reminder is one shared by author Ron Friedman: "Ask yourself this question the moment you sit at your desk – the day is over and I am leaving the office with a tremendous sense of accomplishment. What have I achieved?" The last thing Kenneth Chenault CEO of Amex does before leaving his office is to write down the top three things he wants to accomplish the next morning. Sergey Brin, co-founder of Google, exercises intensely every morning and apparently has a fitness obsession and frequently wooshes around on rollerblades, doing yoga stretches during meetings or walking around on his hands for fun. (You don't have to do that). Steve

Jobs apparently gave himself a motivational speech every morning. He looked in the mirror and asked, "If today was the last day of my life, would I be happy with what I'm about to do today?" If he responded with 'no' too many days in a row, then he knew something needed to change. He also advocated minimalism from furnishing his house to the clothes he wore, and often wore the black t-shirt with blue jeans – to save thinking about options that weren't important.

The practice

- Drinking a glass of warm water with lemon when you first wake up in the morning has a variety of benefits and is an excellent way to get your body kick-started for the day.

- Starting your day well starts the night before. If you habitually stay up past midnight every night, you aren't going to get the rest you need.

- Stretching is a great way to wake up your muscles.

- Turn off all of your electronic gizmos before bed.

- Empty your inbox on a regular basis.

- Determine what will make tomorrow special.

- Too often we live with a time-and-effort mentality. "Well, I worked like stink today – I must have been effective." Not necessarily so. It's not about time and effort. It's about results.

65

LOOK AT THE BIG PICTURE

JUST LIKE A FILM, our lives are composed of a mix of wide-angle shots and detailed close-ups. On a day-to-day basis, your attention is probably on the close-ups: the steps you need to take to move from A to B and on to Z. That's a good thing – this is the level at which work gets done. At times, though, it's helpful that you take a step back and get a bird's eye view and see the wide shot – the big picture.

The idea

There is the 1969 story that when asked by a TV reporter what he did, the NASA washroom janitor replied, "Why, I put a man on the moon." Seeing the big picture implies viewing the whole and not just the (or, most likely, some of the) parts of a process or activity. Visualization, which we've discussed, is where we have a clear and solid picture of what we want and then through focusing on that image we visualize what it would be like to have it. We don't necessarily see all the component parts. A big picture is made up of component parts like a model aircraft or a jigsaw. You don't have to know all the detail necessarily of how each part works, but you do need to know where they go and how they fit. Unpacking your big-picture jigsaw thinking into a handful of specific goals will make it that much more doable.

Having a big picture is an overlay of all the parts including the activity's objectives. Big picture thinking is the way a person looks at problems, opportunities and situations. The big picture is the complete perspective of an issue or a situation.

The best managers are those who can see the big picture, but also who understand the detail of what's required. Anne Mulcahy's efforts to turn Xerox around were successful in part because of her in-depth knowledge of the company's operations; she was especially detail-oriented during the crucial early years of her management when Xerox was close to collapsing.

Big picture thinking means strategic thinking. Often, managers get stuck on tactical details that stall strategic thinking. It's important to check validity by considering our thinking on a micro level – 'how actually would we implement this?', but the big picture is an enabler. In order to see the bigger picture, it's important to allocate time for thinking and kicking ideas around with someone you trust, someone who can perhaps see the bigger picture better than you.

In a 2016 annual letter to shareholders, Amazon's Jeff Bezos provided an example of big picture thinking: "Jeff, what does Day 2 look like? That's a question I just got at our most recent all-hands meeting. I've been reminding people that it's Day 1 for a couple of decades. I work in an Amazon building named Day 1 and, when I moved buildings, I took the name with me... Day 2 is stasis. Followed by irrelevance. Followed by excruciating, painful decline. Followed by death. And that is why it is always Day 1... I'm interested in the question: how do you fend off Day 2? What are the techniques and tactics? How do you keep the vitality of Day 1, even inside a large organization? Such a question can't have a simple answer. There will be many elements, multiple paths and many traps. I don't know the whole answer, but I may know bits of it. Here's a starter pack of essentials for Day 1 defense: customer obsession, a skeptical view of proxies, the eager adoption of external trends, and high-velocity decision making."

Sometimes we make assumptions. Sometimes people tell us what assumptions to have. And we can't be afraid to challenge our own assumptions. Removing assumptions can help us to see the bigger picture. It's also part of generating a positive mindset. We might also challenge the obvious to 'get' the bigger picture. IBM realised that it wasn't a business machine company. It first sold commercial scales and punch card tabulators and, later, mainframe computers. Also, when Paul Buccheit set out to build a new email service at Google, he considered Google's unique perspective. Applying the Google perspective (search) to an old problem (email) created a new solution (Gmail). Nokia started out as a Finnish paper mill, a rubber works and a cable business. GE first began as a way for inventor Thomas Edison to sell his electric inventions, notably the light bulb – and then gas engines, hybrid locomotives, HD CT scanners, ultra-sound devices, chemical sensors. Things change, things develop, markets alter, people see other 'pictures' – whatever the scenario, somebody leading the charge has to see a big picture to make anything work

The practice

- Keep a journal or a plan of all the component parts of any project for which you have responsibility.

- Go on a retreat. Go away to somewhere quiet where you can think, daydream, write, draw... whatever works for you to get any issue clear.

- Attend a conference or a congress. Talk to people in your specialist field (or in the one you want to move into) and learn new ideas.

- Imagine sitting in a room with the people you most admire throughout history. Ask each one: how would you approach a particular problem? (It's good for dinner parties too.)

- Build some model aircraft and complete some complex jigsaws.

DON'T HAVE ANY ATTITUDE OF ENTITLEMENT

THERE'S A PARABLE IN the book *Who Moved My Cheese?* by Spencer Johnson. Two little mice and two miniature people are put in a maze. When the mice discover that the cheese isn't where it's supposed to be, they immediately try to find another piece of cheese. The two miniature people, instead, get angry that the cheese has been moved. They waste time being outraged and blaming each other. They think that they're entitled to the cheese.

The idea

Egnyte's CEO Vineet Jain, is expanding his file-sharing business in other locations because Silicon Valley workers have, according to him, "a sense of entitlement" and competing to hire them is a near-impossible task. Egnyte plans to expand from about 350 employees to 500 globally by hiring from outside the Valley. Workers in the biggest tech hub in the U.S. demand high salaries and big perks – and jump ship if they don't like their work because opportunities are so plentiful. Jain says that this is because there are no consequences for non-performance and that people have a sense of entitlement.

It's one thing to say we want to live life on our own terms. That's empowerment but some people jump right over empowerment and go for entitlement. They demand 'rights', some of which aren't. We can set any (achievable) goals we want, but that's the start only. The hard bit is doing the work necessary to achieve the desired outcome. Not for someone else to deliver it on a plate. People expect respect without giving it. They expect praise and demand sacrifice from others without offering it. Where there has been a culture of entitlement in an organization, the expectation is for things to continue as they always have – because a sense of entitlement embodies within it a definitive 'this is my right' attitude.

People often want to know only what's in it for them. They want the same overtime and time off benefits that they've enjoyed forever. The Millennial obsession with social media, the need for instant gratification and the changing nature of the job market are possibly to blame but the older generation have 'as of right' expectations too. Many people put themselves first. There are some who don't believe that there are alternative views to their own. They not only believe that they're entitled to voice their point of view (fair), but that theirs is the only valid view (unfair).

FedEx used entitlement as a positive. It began as a service for packages that 'absolutely, positively' had to get there overnight. The slogan helped cement the idea that everyone is entitled to instant gratification. Conversely, TV shows celebrate acquisitive and entitled lifestyles. And consider a Burger King slogan 'Have it your way.' Some believe that it encouraged selfishness, leading people to become angry over burgers that arrive with unwanted cheese or sauce. And then there's the matter of seat entitlement on aircraft – where people have been dragged off because of over-booking.

Some entitlement is regarded as a valid 'right' and some as 'selfish'. Some people expect the same rules that apply to others shouldn't apply to themselves. They feel massively put out when other people ask them for help, but expect that when *they* ask for help it should be immediately forthcoming. There are people who expect other people to be more interested in them and what's on their agenda. The opposite doesn't occur to them. These people disregard rules that are intended for everyone's comfort. They ignore signs that tell us not to put feet on train seats. They inconvenience others without thinking. They cancel appointments or reservations repeatedly without thinking about the consequences. They don't buy into the idea of reciprocity. This is all negative and has no relevance to mindset growth.

The practice

- Entitlement should never replace merit.

- Don't demand. Ask. But also give. Your attitude at all times should be: "It's up to me to get what I want and to be what I want to be but I don't need to be selfish to achieve that."

- John Mitchell (the U.S. Attorney General under President Nixon) said: "Our attitude toward life determines life's attitude toward us."

- And Mahatma Gandhi said, "Be the change you wish to see in the world." He never said anything about waiting for someone to hand it to you on a plate.

- Observe what happens when you curb your entitlement tendencies, when you stop thinking of yourself always at the centre of everything.

- Don't take the moral high ground. You can't always justify things that you know are wrong.

- Always remember that the world doesn't owe you anything. There are 7 billion people on the planet. You don't really deserve anything more than any of the others.

67 | BE CONSTRUCTIVE

Of course, being constructive goes hand-in-hand with positivity and growth. Be constructive in your criticism of yourself. Don't be super-critical where nothing is ever good enough, but be both practical and positive in your view of yourself and what you do. This helps shape your opinions and the way you process attitudes.

The idea

Destructive conversations involve blame, complaints, gossip and any shared negativity. They are destructive because they damage and deplete our energy. We may feel an initial rush when we hear about something or someone, but it doesn't really help us in any way. Destructive conversations have no purpose other than to express negativity, waste time and make people feel bad. They may benefit the teller but not you.

People aren't necessarily destructive on purpose. They may have learned it from the organization's culture – its tolerance of negativity through the lack of leadership or, worse, by management's example. Finding an environment where we can make a difference through positive efforts will have a huge impact on our level of happiness. However, if we're part of the problem or, if we believe that by learning new behaviours and learning to speak up, then change starts with us.

The practice

- Constructive conversations are positive, meaningful and beneficial.

- Every time you meet someone, there's an opportunity for the conversation to be destructive or constructive.

- Let people know what you appreciate about them. Constructive environments breed trust. Trust breeds risk-taking and fun.

68

DON'T BELIEVE IN LUCK

PEOPLE WITH A GROWTH mindset are unusually lucky. Or so the media would have us think. Is it a case of being in the right place at the right time? Is it a question of chemistry with someone who employs you over someone else? Maybe luck is just, well, happenchance. Maybe successful people don't have luck necessarily, but just know how to create – and take – advantage of opportunities. Almost everything that happens in life can be traced back to some amount of effort.

The idea

We prefer to focus on positive expectations rather than on drawbacks. While other people see barriers and what ifs, we should see 'why nots' and opportunities. So, part of developing a growth mindset is all about developing a mind that's open to possibilities. Luck, if it exists, is closely related to the concept of chance, but it's not the same. Chance is just what happens, one way or another: the coin coming up heads rather than tails, the dice showing a six, one of the million possible tickets in a lottery. In contrast, luck attaches a value to the outcome of chance. Luck is chance with a layer of good or bad fortune. It's good if you win the lottery and it's bad if you catch a cold.

Chance, then, is the truth or reality we find in random outcomes and luck is a consequence of the value we place on those outcomes. Slipping on ice seems unlucky however you look at it (although next to you in hospital might be the guy who offers you your next peach of a job), whereas it's hard to see winning the lottery as unlucky. So perhaps, we should look for ways to alter the chance, the probability, that different outcomes will occur.

The world is full of beliefs that we can change our chances – and hence our luck. Superstitions are examples: kissing the pitch, putting on your left sock first or taking your favourite pen into the exam. Millions of people experience triskaidekaphobia – a fear of the number 13. While this fear derives from the Last Supper, a New Testament event that is said to have happened 2,000 years ago, its effects are still 'real' to some people. This thinking applies to culture and business too: In Chengdu, apartments on floors with numbers ending in '8' were almost 9 per cent higher in price when resold. Chinese people spend money on acquiring the number '8' for cars and property. The prices of licence plates with '8' are higher at auction than those without.Even the Bank of China is not immune to superstitious influence. It opened its operations in Hong Kong on August 8, 1988; while the Beijing Olympic Games were officially opened at 8:08pm on August 8, 2008. In literature too. luck is honoured. *Adventures of Huckleberry Finn* features Jim telling Huck that hairy arms and a hairy chest are indicators of future wealth.

It's unlikely that any such things increase the chance of a favourable outcome. If you train hard, you're more likely to win a sporting event, but it clearly doesn't explain everything. Your hard work doesn't reduce the chance of being kept awake by noisy neighbours the night before an exam or tripping on the heels of the competitor as you run the race. And people seem to win lotteries regardless of how unpleasant they might be. Our focus should be all about finding opportunities to succeed. That's not necessarily luck.

The practice

- The illusion of luck can consume you if you're not careful.

- Mindset development needs just that – development and, while opportunities will come your way where you can grow faster and maybe better, luck has little to do with it.

- The difference between Bill Gates and similarly advantaged people isn't necessarily luck. Gates went further, taking a confluence of certain circumstances and creating a huge return on opportunities.

- Richard Branson writes, "People and businesses that are generally considered fortunate or luckier than others are usually also the ones that are prepared to take the greatest risks and, by association, are also prepared to fall flat on their faces every so often."

69

LEARN TO NETWORK

Success-oriented people – with a positive outlook – recognize the value of social engagement. They find, and surround themselves with, the kind of people whose talents can complement their own. Successful people align themselves with other people who think like winners.

The idea

Alexander Saint-Amand, CEO of problem-solving consultancy Gerson-Lehrman writes, "I never really liked the word networking. I prefer conversations and teaching." Some view networking in a work environment as insincere at best, manipulative at worst. Lack of confidence, fear of rejection (and a sense of unworthiness) all play their part. You may find that your social graces are limited or that you are scared of gatherings. Well, we need to learn that successful networking is all about some confidence. A good start is to seek out familiar faces. A next step is to find people whom you may know by reputation or because you've had some dealings with them. If a senior someone talks to *you*, don't clam up. Assume that you've been approached for a reason.

Introverts often apologize when asking for an individual's help because they see networking as an imposition, not as an exercise in relationship building. They feel as if they're asking someone to do them a favour. They don't think they're worth someone else's time – so they apologize for it. We don't have to apologize for talking to someone unless we're interrupting. By nature, we're communal, so the shy person isn't shy by nature. The likelihood is that s/he is more concerned about how s/he will seem to others rather than being *interested* in others. Change that and the scenario alters.

In 1936 Dale Carnegie wrote a book (possibly *the* book) on networking. *How to Win Friends and Influence People* demystified the process of making friends out of strangers. There are some simple lessons, the first one of which is to smile. People often just don't think about it and don't realise they're walking around wearing a scowl. Serious expressions are forbidding and make others think that we're unfriendly or unapproachable. People are more likely to warm to someone with a smile than they are to someone with a dour countenance. Obvious? Yet again, yes – but it happens a great deal – as you very well know.

The practice

- In line with overall mindset growth, see networking as an opportunity for discovery and learning, rather than a chore.

- Joining a group engaged in conversation can be awkward. The best way to do this is to pose a question to the group after getting the gist of the conversation. You build your credibility by asking a question and, for a shy person, that's a much easier way to engage than by barging in with an opinion which tends to alienate others.

- You should say the person's name to whom you're speaking without perpetually peering at the name badge.

- Don't be artificial.

- Do some preparation if you know you're likely to meet a particular person.

- After making a new connection, remember to make contact afterwards.

70

DECIDE WHY YOU WANT WHAT YOU WANT

IF YOU'RE FEELING UPSET because you consider that you *aren't* achieving the things you want in life, take a moment to work out the reasons *why* you actually want those things. You may find you're not as attached to them as you think.

The idea

Getting what you want out of life is to some extent determined by what you have decided you *definitely* want – and what you can *really* achieve. Some people are content to let life dictate how it's going to be. That's the fixed mindset way. Yours is becoming, or is, a growth mindset and so you can change and target what you want. We can choose to go for things because they're 'there', but we also need a rationale, a justification, as to why we want them.

Under Mindy Grossman's leadership, Home Shopping Network evolved from a dull shopping outlet to an integrated content TV experience. In an article in *Harvard Business Review*, she talked of her need to focus on what she wanted: "To fix it, I needed to dramatically alter the company's culture. I also needed to understand and reposition the brand and then devise a product strategy that made sense. Not only did I have to do all those things at the same time, but we had to change the tires while the car was running. This was a 24/7 TV operation, so we couldn't close the store while we prepared to relaunch."

The most important principle in achieving any goal is to decide what we think we might want and not immediately focus thoughts on how we'll achieve it. If we concentrate on how something might be done, we can become discouraged, because we either don't know a way of doing it or we don't have the skills required to achieve it. And so, we never get started. We must decide what we want and then why we want it. Or of course that can be reversed. In order to achieve x you may need to have y and in order to have y you need skill z. As Abraham Lincoln said, "You cannot escape the responsibility of tomorrow by evading it today." Alibaba's Jack Ma was the first entrepreneur from China to appear on the cover of Forbes magazine. Before getting accepted to Hangzhou Teacher's Institute, Ma was rejected from university many times. After graduation, he applied for thirty jobs and was turned down for them all. His focus and objective has always been to sell – and nothing else. That's what he wanted.

Society and the media tell us what we should want. Others know what they want us to want. Your family, partner, the company for which you work, religious institutions, politicians and retailers know exactly what they want you to want. These external ideas will accumulate. You need to control what *you* truly want and think. Every entrepreneur has *that* moment – an experience, an epiphany – getting fired, desperate, fed up, lucky enough to have the right mentor – that inspired them to someday become an entrepreneur. Hiten Shah (of analytics businesses KISSmetrics and Crazy Egg) spent $1,000,000 on a web hosting company that was never launched. He is a perfectionist so he built the best thing he could without even understanding what customers wanted. Maybe crazy? It perfected absolute focus – albeit in a costly way, but that's relative. He and his colleagues learned to spend smart, optimize for learning and focus on customer delight. Co-founder Neil Patel says, "... Once I learned to focus all of my time and energy into one business, I was able to make it grow faster than all of my previous businesses."

The practice
- If you are open-minded, aware of your positivity and happy to develop on a continual basis (i.e. to learn and grow), your wants are always going to be more articulate than the ones you inherit from society. They're specific.

- If we encounter too many setbacks in a particular area of life, we tend to stop wanting those things. Ask yourself what you *can't* have and then see if you would want those things if you *could* have them.

- Advertisers (and our families) don't (always) know what we want, but they push ideas at us. You can spend a lot of time pursuing what it is that others think we should want.

- Wrote evangelist Robert H. Schuller, "What would you do if you knew you couldn't fail?"

- Anthony Robbins writes, "Our beliefs are like unquestioned commands, telling us how things are, what's possible and impossible and what we can and cannot do. They shape every action, every thought and every feeling that we experience. As a result, changing our belief systems is central to making any real and lasting change in our lives." Mindset change? Yes indeed.

CHAPTER 8
BE STRONG

71 HAVE SOLUTIONS WHEN POINTING OUT PROBLEMS

BEING A SMARTASS IS no good. Saying that something is wrong or weak is no help if there's no substance behind your comment. You need to be helpful and constructive. That's also a reputation worth having.

The idea

In India, people were pointing out the problem to Richa Kar, but not the solution. So, in 2011 she set up Zivame with the aim of helping women to shop uninhibitedly for intimate wear. Zivame is now well known for producing designer lingerie. Kar believed in providing a service for a product that people wouldn't normally discuss, but which was badly needed.

We can't always deliver fast solutions (although medical people, fire officers, the police and other 'emergency' professions do). There are also some issues to which there is no one solution and the possible solutions are just so huge as are the problems: Mid-East peace, global warming, the future of the Internet, increased longevity and so on. But in everyday personal or business life, there are issues on which we have to – and should – make decisions.

Former astronaut, James Lovell said, "There are people who make things happen, there are people who watch things happen and there are people who wonder what happened. To be successful, you need to be a person who makes things happen." We've all been in a meeting where the participants spend all their time declaring what's wrong with a current situation, but never provide a solution. Maybe you've done it too. These meetings can turn into finger pointing but they don't solve anything. They can be smug witch hunts and are damaging. The key is to define a problem (possibly an opportunity, yes), but then offer a solution or a path to *define* a solution. We mustn't underestimate our own impact on solving problems, but we mustn't overestimate our understanding of the problem. Many people crash straight into discussing something that they don't fully or even partially understand. You, with a growth mindset, will have got your ducks in a line.

The practice

- Successful people are a catalyst. They make things happen. Driven by passion and fuelled by their dreams, they're determined to take informed action and make a difference.

- Suggest and share all consequences of a problem – including your suggestions.

- There may be more than one possible solution to a given issue. These may be better than yours.

- Clarify deadlines by which a solution must be found.

- Can the solution to a problem actually work?

- People are often more than eager to brainstorm with you *what's* wrong, instead of brainstorming the solutions to what's wrong. That way lies blame and attrition.

- Before you bring a problem to a boss or even in a relationship, first think about a viable solution and consequences. Everything has consequences.

BE DECISIVE

WHILE MANY PROCRASTINATE TO the point of inaction, there's a contrasting position: making rash decisions based on emotion. Both are negative. Said Michelle Obama, "You can't make decisions based on fear and the possibility of what might happen." And Peter Drucker wrote, "Whenever you see a successful business, someone once made a courageous decision." You can improve your development no end by being decisive.

The idea

It's much easier to make decisions when we're clear about what we're trying to achieve, why we're trying and how we plan to achieve it. Any decision can have a plus and a minus in its outcome. The result could be this or that. Not all of our decisions are the right ones and that's fine. Waiting and waiting to make a decision (and sometimes not making it) is obviously of no value to the objective and neither is it to the other people involved or you.

Putting off improvement or change because you always find an excuse or reason doesn't add anything. We can fall into the indecision trap by just thinking about one word in our minds: 'later'. As CEO of Alibaba, China's biggest e-commerce company, Daniel Zhang sees it as his duty to only attack the tough decisions. And when it comes to making them, he says acting promptly is more important than always being right: "You can always course-correct if things don't work out. The real fear is in the state of paralysis that results when you can't make a decision at all." The reputation of many business leaders has been marred by decisions made slowly. Take former Blockbuster CEO John Antico, who took a long time to eventually refuse an opportunity to buy Netflix in 2000 for $50 million. He had some reasons for rebuffing Netflix co-founder Reed Hastings' offer, but he still said 'no'. But it was a 'no' long in its coming.

When we seek perfection (even if we don't know what perfection might be) we waste time and that can have consequences. Sometimes we may not want to be rushed when a big decision comes our way. That does *not* mean dithering necessarily. But a decision needs to be made. We can of course break down big decisions into several smaller ones so that we can test, evaluate and modify. A good start can be made by evaluating the worst that could happen. And the best.

The practice

- The stakes may be high with some decisions and you're right to be concerned about making the best decision possible.

- Don't pontificate too long.

- Be sure that you're not mistakenly rationalizing one option over others due to unwarranted fear, peer pressure or unfounded fantasy.

- Let options percolate in your mind as you take stock. Go for a walk. If time allows. Talk to people and then be alone.

- If an option requires you to compromise your integrity, don't just jettison your beliefs.

- Sometimes the right choice is the brave choice.

73 FEEL COMFORTABLE IN YOUR OWN SKIN

To MAKE ANY DEEP change, you have to like yourself. Being comfortable with yourself means not comparing yourself to others; it means feeling OK with whatever choices you make in life. It can also mean acceptance of what you're becoming.

The idea

When we're truly comfortable with ourselves, we don't feel the need for comparisons and we don't feel the need to do things simply to impress others. And yet, getting to this point can take work. Especially with the constant barrage from social media and advertising of the so-called perfect life that can make us feel like our own isn't up to par. Inevitably someone else's day looks better and suddenly we feel incomplete. The best cure for this is to become authentic.

Authentic living correlates with happiness – subjective and psychological well-being. It also means being the real you. When we have the courage to live authentically, we feel better. See how Polonius' advice to his son Laertes in Shakespeare's *Hamlet* reflects authentic living, "This above all: to thine ownself be true, And it must follow, as the night the day, Thou canst not then be false to any man."

One way to figure out who we really are is by doing things that make us happy. When we're feeling less than good about ourselves, it's easy to get into negativity. The negativity shows and it's not appealing. Sure, it's good to embrace our so-called flaws (of which we all have some). It's easier said than done. Everyone has something they don't like about themselves, but those so-called flaws are often what makes us unique, memorable and liked.

Being comfortable with yourself, both physically and emotionally, takes practice and time. Self-like is the fastest route to literally anything we want. We have to believe that we deserve to be happy and successful, however we define what that means. It's an immutable fact – feel good about you and you'll feel better about whatever you set out to do.

Taking full responsibility for the life you've created for yourself – or the life you're in the process of creating – is hugely empowering. This also means that you don't have to tolerate what you choose not to tolerate. That of course is a big statement because sometimes we have to tolerate things. Tolerating anything sucks the life out of you. We sometimes confuse tolerance with acceptance. There are some things we must accept but few we have to tolerate.

The practice

- Back to where we began – focus on the deliberate rewiring of your belief system because you know that your beliefs are determining everything you experience. It'll be like a refreshing wash.

- If you aren't living the life you want, take steps (if relevant) to discover which of your beliefs are keeping you from it.

- It's easier to feel good about who you are when you look after yourself.

- Once you've realised the real you – embrace the real you.

- You have to find time for yourself. No distractions, no chatting, no email, no Twitter – just you, your thoughts, and (hopefully) a sense of comfort.

- You are spectacular.

BUILD TRUST

ALL SUCCESSFUL RELATIONSHIPS RUN on trust. With trust, all things are possible: progress, productivity and ingenuity. Commitment, engagement, loyalty and excellence become more than empty words in a mission statement; they become a reality. Trust is a bonding agent that holds everything together in relationships and you need to trust and be trusted. Once broken, trust can't be easily fixed.

The idea

Motivational public speaker, Brian Tracy, said, "The glue that holds all relationships together – including the relationship between the leader and the led – is trust and trust is based on integrity."

The 168 million registered eBay users are mostly strangers to each other, yet they engage in one million financial transactions every day. According to former eBay CEO Meg Whitman, "I still believe... the fundamental reason eBay worked was that people everywhere are basically good." Well, some might disagree and consider greed and avarice a part of the process. As we become more interconnected, concern about the business trust gap will grow.

John C. Havens is co-author (with Shel Holtz) of the book, *Tactical Transparency: How Leaders Can Leverage Social Media to Maximize Value and Build their Brand*. He argues that the market and customers will increasingly demand that companies become more transparent – and punish those that fail to do so. Most businesses have a strong corporate purpose and profess to build trust. Their organizational values, cultures and behaviour try to reflect that trust. That's hard and takes little to breach.

In 2002, Arthur Andersen, Enron, WorldCom and other companies cast a veil of suspicion across American business. Trust and its breach became news. Breaching trust breaks businesses. Lehman Investment Bank, with $600 billion in assets, failed in late 2008. It was the largest bankruptcy ever and lit the worldwide financial crisis fire. There were claims against its top executives and its auditor, Ernst & Young, for fraud. Enron's bankruptcy in 2001, after allegations of massive accounting fraud, wiped out $78 billion in stock market value and led to the collapse of Arthur Andersen. And so on.

In 2017, and according to consultancy firm Great Place to Work, Google's employees in Argentina thought Google was a great place to work mostly because of trust. The same was found in Google offices in Brazil, Canada, India, Switzerland and the U.S. When businesses effectively articulate their purpose, act transparently and stand by their values, trust and success can go hand in hand. "Fulfilling our potential," writes Simon Sinek, "has something to do with us and everything to do with building trust with the people around us." The same is true of any business.

The practice

- Ethical behaviour is as simple as living up to your stated values. And only you can define what those values are.

- Trust helps employees be more accepting of change.

- Trust works both ways. Once it's gone, it's usually gone for good. At home and at the office.

- Be transparent and keep your promises.

75 HAVE COURAGE

FROM GEORGE R.R. MARTIN's, *A Game of Thrones*: "Bran thought about it. 'Can a man still be brave if he's afraid?' 'That is the only time a man can be brave,' his father told him." Change requires courage. Mindset change requires courage. But if you want to change, you must be willing to feel the discomfort of resisting your ego and beating any fears you may have.

The idea

Wrote Richard Branson, "My success has been driven by courage to try. I'm not the bravest or smartest person, but I'm courageous enough to dream big, challenge myself and take bold risks." In order to change, we need the courage to break the beliefs that no longer serve us or in which we no longer have empathy. Courage means being afraid – and acting anyway. If we tend to be fearful, we probably assume that we're not courageous. Wrong. Courage is doing tough things and sometimes doing things that are hard. There's the Kennedy line,"We choose to go to the moon in this decade and do the other things, not because they are easy, but because they are hard."

Feeling afraid and acting anyway takes courage. We aren't born courageous, so we shouldn't expect to magically acquire it without work. However, it doesn't always come to the fore until really pushed and, even then, sometimes it doesn't. Which is why we're open-mouthed in awe at those who show courage in extraordinary circumstances. There are other measures of courage: asking someone out for a date, standing up for someone or to a bully, asking for a promotion, leaving an abusive relationship, making a presentation.

We have beliefs – possibly some of yours have changed by now – and these beliefs must be reinforced, sometimes explained and often defended. That takes courage. Charles Darwin wrote, "A shy man no doubt dreads the notice of strangers, but can hardly be said to be afraid of them. He may be as bold as a hero in battle and yet have no self-confidence about trifles in the presence of strangers." Well, it's easier to be courageous on behalf of others than it is for our own sake. It's hard, for example, to be a lone voice.

From religious texts to fairy tales, from ancient myths to Hollywood movies, cultures worldwide are rich with tales of courage. From the cowardly lion in *The Wizard of Oz* who finds the courage to face the witch to *Star Wars or Harry Potter*, we're raised on a diet of heroic and inspirational stories. Yet courage is not just physical bravery. Social activists like Martin Luther King and Nelson Mandela, were courageous. Mandela wrote, "I learned that courage was not the absence of fear, but the triumph over it. The brave man is not he who does not feel afraid, but he who conquers that fear."

Olivia Lum started Hyflux in Singapore with next to nothing selling water treatment systems. Now it's one of Asia's leading water and fluid treatment companies. For 15 years, James Dyson tried to build a better vacuum cleaner, scrapping a reported 5,127 prototypes in total. He says that each prototype brought him one step closer to perfection.

We need the courage to be different and make different choices with no guarantees for how others will respond. We often hold back and don't do or say what needs to be said or done because we're fearful. Take courage. A piece from Tolkien's The Hobbit: "'Go back?' he thought. 'No good at all! Go sideways? Impossible! Go forward? Only thing to do! On we go!' So up he got, and trotted along with his little sword held in front of him and one hand feeling the wall, and his heart all of a patter and a pitter."

The practice

- Find role models. When you're trying to stretch yourself beyond your apparent limits, there's a part of you that wonders whether it can actually be done. A role model is a reminder that the answer is 'yes'.

- Read. Gain knowledge. Knowing something and having a credible source will build your confidence about what you know to be true.

- Determine what exactly your fear is and face up to it.

- Don't over-analyze. When we start analyzing, we welcome self-doubt which erodes our self-confidence – and courage.

76 · FACE YOUR DEMONS

'FACING YOUR DEMONS' IS a term well known to the introspective person. In facing our demons, we become aware of our subconscious and how it can sabotage our lives. The problem with facing our demons is that we have to find them first. Often, we're totally unaware of them. Anything which holds us back from any growth needs to be managed – and promptly.

The idea

Facing our demons is something we all have to do at some point. We must confront the things that really worry us – our insecurities, shortcomings, deep secrets, things we've done, things that were done to us and the suspicion that maybe we're not as good as we pretend. Taking stock of ourselves – and being 100 per cent honest with what we find – is a necessity.

Society puts a premium on perfection. This often keeps us from digging beneath our own surfaces. And so, instead, we don't deal with demons. We need to become aware of the repressed parts of our personalities. Most people don't face their demons until they're at their lowest ebb.

Avoidance is a problem. We must find a way to reconnect or move on to something that excites us. Prevarication on this can be a demon too. Fear of failure raises its head again here. Feeling that we're not good enough is a demon. "Whether you think you can, or you think you can't, you're right," wrote Henry Ford. And the monsters don't disappear by ignoring them. If only. In fact, these issues only escalate when neglected. They manifest themselves in crooked, twisted ways, creeping into our work, relationships, anxieties, dreams and sense of peace. So, we must confront the parts of ourselves that we prefer would just disappear. We need to shed light on them. It takes courage. You may have to forgive yourself or forgive others or come to terms with something that happened but that which you can't alter.

It is said that when the Buddha was under the Bodhi tree seeking enlightenment, the demons came. He tried to fight them off for days. Finally, realizing that, at best, they would reach an impasse, he invited them to sit with him. Painful in the extreme maybe and not always 100 per cent possible but still, facing those things that hurt can be calming and allow you to change. By inviting your demons 'to tea', you establish ownership of your shadow.

The practice

- Face your demons now. Seek help if necessary. If you keep trying to bury them, you feed each one.

- Look ahead. Take a look around the nooks and crannies of your past that have left you feeling less than happy. Give them what they need to heal and move on.

- You probably do have the courage to face whatever it is that's tremendously painful.

FIND THE STRENGTH TO SLOW DOWN

IN THE FAST LANE, we're often afraid to slow down – at work and at home. We feel guilty if we take time out to just be. This isn't what life's about, to feel rushed and panicked on a daily basis. And it doesn't help you to grow emotionally or in mindset terms, so slow down.

The idea

According to psychological research conducted at Pittsburgh's Carnegie Mellon University, stress has increased over the past 25 years. That's no surprise. This is due, in large part, to people feeling the need to rush to keep up with an endless supply of new information, new technology and new forms of workplace competition. Stressing ourselves out will only make work – and life – less productive and less fun. Some patience is necessary for slowing down, but patience is a hard master or mistress. So, understand where your impatience comes from. We live in a world where we're expected to keep moving – meetings, more meetings, appointments, reports, collecting, delivering, continual time management. People complain about lateness, over-running and being frantically busy. Some see this a virtue. It isn't. Slowing down from time to time is important for growth, but requires strength of character to make it happen.

Professors Kimberly Elsbach and Andrew Hargadon have suggested that we balance our workday activities with a mix of 'mindful' (cognitively demanding) and 'mindless' (cognitively facile) activities. Giving the mind a rest from high level responsibilities and doing simple (but necessary) administrative tasks, give us freedom to take control of our schedules and maintain momentum with less strain.

Mark Williams, professor of clinical psychology at Oxford University, says working in a culture where stress is a badge of honour is counterproductive, "We can spend so much time rushing from one task to another. We may think we're working more efficiently, but as far as the brain is concerned, we are working against the grain. No wonder we get exhausted." The neurological benefits of mindfulness (focusing one's awareness on the present moment), have been linked to an increase in emotional intelligence, specifically empathy.

Google, Apple, General Mills, Aetna and AstraZeneca, among others, have implemented mindfulness programmes. They report improvements in focus, attention and memory. Working mindfully involves resisting distractions, like checking tweets or emails. Mindfulness teaches us how to notice when we're zoning out and how to bring our minds back to the task at hand. Multi-tasking is harmful to productivity and mindfulness is the opposite of multi-tasking. By focusing on one thing at a time, people slow down, make fewer errors, pay more attention to details and finish work faster.

Slowing down allows us to be more present and aware in the company of others, enjoying relationships in a different way. When we're so busy, we run the risk of becoming physically and emotionally exhausted, which in turn causes high levels of anxiety and stress. Eating slowly, talking slower, driving more slowly or catching the later, less crowded train will help create calm.

The practice
- Do less. It's hard to slow down when you're trying to do a million things. Focus on what *really* needs to be done.

- Being connected all the time means we're constantly stressed about incoming information and are at the mercy of the demands of others. So, disconnect sometimes. You'll lose nothing and gain a lot.

WALK AND TALK

WALKING AND TALKING WITH someone, or several people, helps problem-solving and lessens chances of procrastination. This way of meeting requires (and gives) focus, strength of mind and commitment.

The idea

Steve Jobs, Richard Branson, Mark Zuckerberg, Twitter's Jack Dorsey and Barack Obama have been advocates of 'walk and talk' – although fans of the US political drama *The West Wing*, with which the term is closely associated, might recall that POTUS's staff actually called it a 'pedeconference'. A 2014 study by Stanford University found a person's creative output increased on average by 60 per cent when walking. Aristotle allegedly taught while strolling about, which fits with his students being called Peripatetics.

Walking is a good way to release endorphins, a set of feel-good chemicals that dull pain receptors in the brain, sedate us and give us feelings of euphoria. Jack Groppel, vice-president of Wellness & Prevention, a consulting group owned by Johnson & Johnson, has advocated a programme that calls for standing up and walking around in the workplace for one or two minutes every half hour, a process that he says increases productivity.

Interviews can beneficially take place whilst walking. Walking allows for the thought process to calm and it means that we don't have to look at someone all of the time, which can be distracting. Walking is a bonding thing too and adopting walking meetings not only benefits us physically and mentally, but it also makes us feel just a little less guilty when later at home we relax with a glass of Pinot and watch the latest episode of *Game of Thrones*.

The practice

- Walking side by side reinforces the perspective that you and others are working on something together.

- If you need or want a serious one-on-one with someone, walking meetings help.

- Imagine the anxiety that often accompanies an unexpected call to meet in your boss's office versus your boss asking you to join him/her on a walk. Difficult conversations happen much more successfully this way.

- Walking keeps you focused and positive. And you take in a different environment.

TEAMWORK WORKS

We've talked about how you will need others to support your quest for a growth mindset. That can be one person or a few (it'll never be many). But teamwork is essential in developing ideas and the self. It promotes selflessness both key to positivity and your personal ambition.

The idea

We probably all know that, by working together, we can produce better results than any of us can usually achieve alone. Heavy equipment company, Caterpillar, believes in making teamwork work and always has. People share talents. The diverse thinking and decision-making of its people strengthens the overall team. Respect and value of people is the number one value. The second is that people strive to understand the overall picture, then do his or her part. At ConocoPhillips, management encourages a can-do spirit to deliver top performance. That involves a fervent belief in collaboration, teamwork and celebration of team success.

Without teamwork, few organizations can succeed. Belonging to a team, in the broadest sense, is a result of feeling part of something larger than ourselves. It has a lot to do with our understanding of objectives. In a team-oriented environment, we contribute to the overall success of the organization. We work with fellow members of an organization to produce understood results. Even though we have a specific job function and we belong to a particular department, we're unified with others to achieve something specific. This is key; the objectives have to be highly specific, otherwise people will have different visualizations of what has to be done.

Team leaders often fail to define the team they want to build. The team skills must be defined and it may be that some skills are missing. These have to be acknowledged and solutions found. Otherwise the team will likely fail.

An organization must demonstrate constancy of purpose in supporting a team with resources of people, time and money. Does the work of the team receive sufficient emphasis as a priority in terms of the time, discussion and attention? Is the direction a mark of real leadership? Does the team understand where its work fits in the total context of the organization's goals? This is no time for woolly garbage. Precision is key. Do team members feel the team mission is important? Are members committed to accomplishing the mission and expected outcomes? Do people perceive their service as valuable to the organization and to their own careers? Do they expect their skills to develop? Are they excited by the opportunity? And is the team empowered to do what it agrees will accomplish its aims? At the same time, do team members understand their boundaries? And, rather important, does the organization understand what the team is doing?

Remember this quote from Henry Ford, "Coming together is a beginning. Keeping together is progress. Working together is success."

The practice

- Fully understand why a team, your team, exists.

- Are you able to manage creative thinking, unique solutions and new ideas?

- Are there rewards or recognition when your team is successful?

- Everyone in your team including you should be able to say, "It's clear. I see it." No one should be questioning the team's objectives or needing to understand what the real meaning behind it is.

- Teamwork and its application is as much a factor of home and family life as it is in business.

BE DISCIPLINED

80

"WITH SELF-DISCIPLINE, ALMOST ANYTHING is possible," wrote Theodore Roosevelt. Self-discipline is one of the greatest obstacles in preventing most people from achieving the levels of success they want. Discipline is the most challenging habit towards consistent delivery.

The idea

Being disciplined isn't something you have – it's something you do. There are many important qualities that can contribute to a person's achievements and happiness, but there is only one that achieves sustainable, long-term success in all aspects of life: self-discipline. People with high self-control are more capable of dealing with goal conflicts. These people are able to make positive decisions more easily. The self-disciplined don't allow their choices to be dictated by impulses or feelings.

In 1836 general of the Texan army, Sam Houston, retreated from the Mexican army. Although his men wanted to fight the Mexicans led by Santa Anna, Houston wouldn't risk their lives. Despite accusations of cowardice, he would not budge. Houston withdrew with discipline even when many doubted him. His discipline proved right when the Texan army eventually defeated the Mexicans in 18 minutes at San Jacinto. The resounding victory was an irreversible blow to the Mexican army and that sowed the seeds for Texan independence.

People like Jack Welch and Richard Branson display or displayed self-declared discipline on a daily basis. They regard discipline as a habit. Charles Duhigg, author of *The Power of Habit*, explains that habits are traced to a part of the brain associated with emotions, patterns, and memories; it's called the basal ganglia. Decisions and disciplines, on the other hand, are made in the prefrontal cortex, a completely different area. When a behaviour becomes habitual, we stop using our decision-making skills and instead function on auto-pilot. Therefore, breaking a bad habit and building a new one not only requires us to make active decisions, it also feels wrong. Our brains will resist the change in favour of what it has been programmed to do. The solution? We must focus hard on the change we want to make. It won't happen on its own. Opinions, views, habits, outlook, learning, disciplines and mindsets all require purpose and effort. Acknowledge that it will take a while for your new regime to feel right or good or natural. Keep chugging along. It will happen.

The practice

- Inspiration is fleeting, emotional and unpredictable. It feels great, but accomplishes little without discipline. If you initially feel inspired you might not complete the task without disciplined action.

- Instituting a new way of thinking won't always go according to plan. You will have ups and downs, fabulous successes and flat failures. The key is to keep moving.

- When you have a setback, acknowledge what caused it and manage accordingly. It's easy to get wrapped up in guilt, anger or frustration, but these won't help improve self-discipline.

- Since 40 per cent of our behaviour is habit-driven, if you want to control your ability to be self-disciplined, you have to control your habits.

- Commitment is the offspring of values. If you can't discipline yourself to do something every day, there's only one explanation: it's simply not that important to you.

CHAPTER 9
LEADERSHIP

DON'T FEAR SUCCESS

81

LEADERS ARE MADE, NOT born. Everyone with a growth mindset, whatever age and circumstance, is capable of self-transformation. Not that everyone will become a leader. Most managers and even CEOs become bosses, not leaders. They wield power instead of transforming themselves, their workers and their organizations.

The idea

Fear of success comes in many guises: fear of failure, fear of inadequacy, fear of the market or competition, fear of leadership, fear of ridicule and so on. Success means change (even if it's the change you always wanted). Fears of success tend to cluster around several issues. One of the core fears that arise from change is that success will lead to isolation. Achieving success means putting yourself out there to be scrutinized and criticized and exposing yourself to new pressures and demands. It's only normal to wonder whether you'll be up to the challenge. A small part of you would rather not take the risk.

When they first become managers, most people enter a period of learning. They (should) get training and coaching; they're open to ideas and they think long and hard about how to do their jobs. They want to develop and of course achieve. But once they've learned the basics, many stop trying to improve. It may seem like too much trouble or they may not see where improvement will take them. They're content to do their jobs rather than making themselves into leaders. They're comfortable where they are. Fixed. Nothing wrong with that of course but you probably don't want that. So, embrace the idea of success.

Great leaders are governed by growth mindsets. Growth mindset people understand that failure is part of the process that guarantees deeper learning and success. Growth mindset leaders understand that harnessing failure can be a recipe for success. They embrace success too. At the age of 15, in 2007, David Karp dropped out of school and developed Tumblr in his bedroom. He sold the blog-hosting company to Yahoo for $1.1 billion in 2013, when his net worth reportedly exceeded $200 million. He simply believed in what he could achieve and in success. His belief was authentic. If we want to succeed, we must stamp out negative beliefs that might be holding us back. People have a tendency to self-handicap. Someone who believes he won't meet sales goals is more likely to prioritize other tasks, giving him an excuse for a poor performance. His belief becomes a self-fulfilling prophecy.

Mark Zuckerberg runs a public company with a market cap of more than $400 billion. Nearly 2 billion users visit his site monthly. He's more afraid of missing out on the opportunity he has to change the world, "I am much more motivated by making sure we have the biggest impact on the world than by building a business or making sure we don't fail. I have more fear in my life that we aren't going to maximize the opportunity that we have than that we mess something up and the business goes badly." The lesson is apt: seeking opportunities will get us further in business than trying to avoid mistakes.

The practice

- Don't be afraid to share good news. It's fine to mention your accomplishments. But without arrogance.

- Growth mindset leaders demonstrate that a love of challenge, an appreciation of effort, a willingness to collaborate and embrace a 'win' are key requirements for success.

- You need to *actively* demonstrate a growth mindset in everything that you say and do, from setting out a vision for success to the way in which you interact with your people once success is achieved.

STRONG LEADERSHIP STARTS WITH AN OPEN MIND

OPEN MINDEDNESS IS THE willingness to consider opposing or contradictory views. Be receptive to fresh ideas, even if those ideas challenge your current strongly held beliefs. You may not always be right.

The idea

People with an open mind are willing to admit that they can be wrong. On the other hand, people with closed minds don't contemplate ideas that contradict their fundamental beliefs. Instead they reject input that challenges their point of view and gather input which supports it. Not healthy. Most people believe that they're open minded, but that's the first belief that they need to challenge. Open-minded people are comfortable with a degree of ambiguity and the unknown; certainly, the new. And their behaviour encourages discovery. Laszlo Bock, SVP of People Operations at Google in 2017 puts it well, "What we've seen is that the people who are the most successful here, who we want to hire, will have a fierce position. They'll argue like hell. They'll be zealots about their point of view. But then you say, 'here's a new fact,' and they'll go 'Oh, well, that changes things; you're right.'"

Jim Kouzes and Barry Posner put it well in their book *The Leadership Challenge* when they wrote: "Titles don't make you a leader. It's how you behave that makes the difference. Exemplary leaders know that if they want to gain commitment and achieve the highest standards, they must be models of the behavior they expect of others." Our mindsets are so influential because they determine how we think about and interpret situations, our emotional reactions, the decisions we make and the actions we take. Our mindsets directly impact the quality of our relationships, the interactions we have and the way we lead. To be open-minded means removing any personal bias and prejudice from any situation.

It is said that, in 1994, before the Internet was off and away, Jeff Bezos found a statistic that said the Internet was growing 2,300 per cent a year. Instead of laughing, he wondered what sort of business opportunity might that mean. He had a blank sheet of paper and considered many options. The world's biggest book shop was born. Since we've been more or less indoctrinated since birth with everything we currently know, becoming and staying open-minded involves practice. We must put ourselves in another person's shoes, allowing ourselves to see things from his/her point of view – and that takes time, energy, and patience. Of course, open-mindedness doesn't even mean that you agree with something. It means you're willing to adjust your own conclusions and take someone else's into consideration when giving a verdict.

The practice

- Always be curious.

- When in a discussion consider both points of view, no matter how difficult that is.

- Respect others' beliefs no matter what. It doesn't mean that you have to agree with them. "I do not agree with what you say, but I'll defend to the death your right to say it." Not Voltaire, but Evelyn Beatrice Hall.

- Good leaders are magnets for people they want to attract. They cultivate enthusiasm, possibility and the wow factor in their relationships, which also encourages the desire for others to join in. Alas, evil people can achieve the same.

83. DEVELOP A MINDSET CULTURE

MOST LEADERS KNOW THAT agility, innovation and collaboration are vital to achieving their goals. Organizational culture is key in determining an organization's success. Since culture is a reflection of leadership, it's critical for leaders to know how they can shift mindset to ensure that everyone in their teams has a positive one.

The idea

According to research by Carol Dweck at Stanford University, people working in growth mindset-orientated companies are 47 per cent more likely to say that their colleagues are trustworthy and 34 per cent more likely to feel a strong sense of ownership and commitment to the organization. Firms which exhibit a growth mindset are recognizable by certain cultural characteristics. Their employees are 65 per cent more likely to say that the organization supports risk-taking and 49 per cent more likely to claim that their organization supports innovation.

In the mid 1990s, IBM had become complacent, narrowly focused on products it already offered and on customers it already served. In other words, it continued to do what had once made it successful. But it was stuck. Lack of innovation, zero forward thinking and a fixed mindset almost cost IBM its existence. The US economy had globalized and the world had become faster-moving. The company started encouraging its employees to be more innovative. Had it failed to evolve, had it not invested in adapting and developing its business, it wouldn't have survived. Today, it's again considered a major player and has global presence. They ditched the ranking system that labelled some employees as stars – a system that critics say hindered collaboration and risk-taking. There's now a culture of learning, teamwork and a growth mindset.

Developing a growth mindset necessitates a focus on results and also on the process by which to achieve those results – something that managers sometimes ignore or assume that it's someone else's task. Focusing on a process encourages people to try new things and seek support in developing those things.

Of all the changes Lou Gerstner found necessary when he became CEO of IBM, culture was the hardest. He wanted to focus on strategy, analysis and measurement. In his book, *Who Says Elephants Can't Dance*, he writes: "Culture isn't just one aspect of the game – it *is* the game. In the end, an organization is nothing more than the collective capacity of its people to create value. Vision, strategy, marketing, financial management – any management system, in fact – can set you on the right path and carry you for a while. But no enterprise... will succeed over the long haul if those elements aren't part of its DNA." Culture is not one of those soft matters to be dealt with when the real business is done. Culture is the style, beliefs and mores by which an organization behaves. Much like a mindset, it can be positive. Or not.

The practice
- Your growth mindset will help you to approach learning new information and skills with a different attitude and enthusiasm.

- Tell success, learning and change stories, celebrating your mistake of the week or rewarding efforts – yours and others'.

- Make it safe to take risks – and make mistakes. Celebrate 'aha' moments. They're just as important as 'wow' moments.

- If there was one action you could take to cultivate more of a growth mindset today for yourself or your team, what would that action be? And if there was a thing that you could change today at your office, what would that be?

INNOVATION IS PART OF LEADERSHIP

WHO WOULD HAVE THOUGHT that cell phones would become cameras and music players? Who would have thought that ordinary, non-technical people would connect globally with their phones? Innovation isn't only about new technology and its adoption. It's also about making work easier – and better – with a bearing on customer satisfaction – internally and externally. This is an attitude, a mindset.

The idea

Innovative leadership inspires others to think outside the box, then creates an environment where new ideas can be tested and evaluated. These leaders tend to be visionaries and motivate their followers through leading by example and collaboration. Innovation can become part of the norm.

Marc Benioff is the founder and CEO of Salesforce.com, a cloud-based company started in 1999. The company expanded through a large number of acquisitions. In 2013, its revenue topped $3 billion. It topped the Forbes World's Most Innovative Companies list in 2011, 2012, and 2013. Salesforce.com claims to have transformed the enterprise software market through innovative expansion and attitude. Swedish run Spotify's success is due to increasingly sophisticated data collection and innovation allowing it to release new products that captivate its users around a particular moment in time rather than offering the same tired genres. Spotify has proved that people will pay for convenient, one–stop access to their tunes – all in the face of Apple Music.

Creative thinking and collaboration can be encouraged and rewarded. It's a leader's job to get it right. It's also very dangerous for any organization to believe that it is too big to waste time on small ideas or that its people are not paid to be creative.

Unlike most organizations that separate individuals into silos (such as marketing versus engineering), innovative enterprises build teams that morph as new processes and ideas unfold: Netflix, Snap, Microsoft, Google, Huawei, Alibaba are some examples. They mix up teams and there are no silos. Some car manufacturers do this now too and it results in a 360-degree focus during ideas' creation with a shared and visualized objective in mind.

An innovative culture is about cultivating a mindset to learn to see the world in new ways. But, innovation isn't neat and tidy. By its very nature, innovation is unpredictable, even though business requires predictability. Innovation is full of surprises as is all creativity. And, frequently, innovation delivers more failure than success, even when our future demands a track record of success. Innovation is intrinsically a contradiction, offering significant improvement to our business, just as it offers up disruption and change.

It's strange isn't it, that positioning innovation as a core value is a high-reward, high-risk proposition? And that means that creating an innovative culture may require a different approach to leadership and a different way of thinking about ourselves. Innovation requires a certain type of person: passionate explorers in pursuit of endless possibilities. Take Tesla's Elon Musk whose motor venture nearly ran out of cash; he invested more of his own money and sold his vision to new investors who committed to multi-year contracts. For Musk, it's the trust he has in his team that keeps his innovations alive – and the faith that investors have in him.

The practice
- Don't stifle any attempt to do something differently.
- Try and banish silos.

- Analytical leaders are clear thinkers. Conceptual leaders are the visionary leaders. You may need to be a bit of both.

- Innovation has a creative culture-empowering effect, telling the team to dream big. Don't let anything stop you from thinking big.

- It's not until you begin to trust yourself and others that real collaboration works.

- You, as an innovative manager, are sincere, unafraid to be yourself and admit when you don't have all the answers.

85 LOOK AT AUTHENTIC LEADERS AND WHAT THEY HAVE IN COMMON

You HAVE MOST LIKELY heard the word authentic used in conjunction with leadership. This is something you should care about as you develop yourself as a leader. Authentic leadership is genuine leadership. Shakespeare wrote in *Hamlet*, "To thine own self, be true." To become an authentic leader, you should do the same.

The idea

In 2006, Alan Mulally arrived as the new CEO of Ford. Allegedly, he immediately asked to meet workers in the main factory. "I'm sorry", a colleague told him, "but Ford executives don't talk directly to factory employees." Mulally was amazed, but insisted on going to the factory floor where he spoke to the workers about their dreams, his hopes for the company and Ford's values. Over the next few years, he transformed Ford from the brink of bankruptcy to an $8 billion profit. As he said in 2013, "Leadership is being authentic to who you are, thinking about what you really believe in and behaving accordingly."

Authenticity has become the gold standard for leadership. No longer is leadership about charisma or looking good. Leadership is about inspiring and empowering those you lead. Authentic leaders have discovered their direction and align people around shared values and direction. Warren Buffett displays authentic leadership in showing a commitment to improving stakeholder value. By stakeholders, include shareholders, employees, customers, the community, the markets. He's an independent thinker who challenges the conventionally accepted way of looking at things and explains his reasoning in a simple way. Chairman Ratan Tata of the Tata Group is the epitome of authentic leadership because he has made an Indian business a global business while keeping his promises, balancing profits and championing CSR.

We want to be led by real people, not figureheads or gods. As our organizations become less hierarchical, we want leaders to whom we can relate. As a leader, the only way we can achieve this is to be ourselves. Pretence can be seen and then no trust exists. Authentic leaders know how to inspire trust. And they prioritize the building of trust *first*. Authentic leaders speak candidly, as Ann Mulcahy did – telling her Xerox team members in 2001 when the business was a gnat's wing from disaster, "Hey, no games. Let's just talk." Leaders like her create a compelling direction for people to follow. They know how to align the organization to get the results they want (and need). They actively cultivate a sense of vitality. They are obsessed with keeping people engaged. And they help create and then defend a company's values.

Great leaders build trust by honouring all stakeholders, doing what they say they're going to do, displaying character and competence – and upholding ethical standards. Today's employees are motivated by more than money (although that matters); they want to know that their work each day matters too.

GM's bankruptcy was really the result of a steady decline over 50 years. When the end came in early 2009, President Obama had the courage to finance the company to bring it out of bankruptcy. And he appointed Ed Whitacre as CEO. Whitacre's leadership turned GM round. His one-year tenure saw a shift from the old way of doing business. He abandoned the aged committee system that protected executives from being accountable for results and made clear, decisive decisions while challenging people to go faster and better. Whitacre even appeared in GM ads, challenging customers to give GM cars a try while offering them their money back if they weren't satisfied. Since turning over the CEO reins to successor Dan Akerson, Whitacre has received undeserved criticism for stepping down. But this was his intention. He noted, "It was my plan – to help return this company to greatness – and not stay a day beyond that." Everyone saw him as authentic.

Authentic leaders confront facts facing them and their organization. They question assumptions. They build an aspirational and achievable plan for progress. They dispel ambiguity and, above all, they communicate well. Great leaders know that they won't have a motivated team unless they themselves exhibit a positive attitude.

The practice

- Getting promoted to a managerial position doesn't automatically turn you into a leader. That takes more work.

- If you listen and learn consistently and develop the right mindset, you can be a good leader.

- There's no greater motivation than seeing the boss alongside everyone else, showing that hard work is being done on every level – as long as it's real work that the boss is doing. If the boss is you, by proving your commitment to the brand and your role, you'll earn the respect of your team and instill that same hardworking energy among your staff.

- Keep your promises.

- Encourage others to develop a growth mindset and a positive outlook.

- You may be forced at times to deviate from your set course. Be strong and tell people what, why and how.

KNOW HOW GREAT LEADERS MEASURE SUCCESS

86

LEADERSHIP ON ITS OWN is meaningless without measurement. Obviously. Or is it obvious? Many so-called leaders measure little. Measurement is mission critical, otherwise you can't plan and grow.

The idea

Results are the main driver when it comes to any business measurement. That usually implies financial results, but it's not only that. It's also other things like skills' improvement and product. Management guru, Peter Drucker, famously wrote, "If you can't measure it, you can't improve it."

Amazon's Jeff Bezos is a leader. He measures his success at running the biggest shop in the world, by focusing on his long-term goal and ignoring critics who tried and try to distract him. His measurement has always been the achievement of what he's promised – whatever it is – internally and externally. Martin Luther King, Jr. was passionate about the African-American civil rights cause. Like Gandhi he advocated non-violence. The thing that made King such a great leader (and by his own measurement) was his ability to inspire people to join his cause. We can be passionate and have great visions for the future, but if we don't know how to inspire people, then not much will happen.

Bill Gates founded Microsoft with Paul Allen in 1987. At the age of 31, Gates was named the world's youngest self-made billionaire. Although his business methods have been criticized as being monopolistic, he's not only a philanthropist, but also a leader. He's not known for having a magnetic personality. Instead, he exudes an air of authority, expertise and credibility. And shares it all with his people. Success in his world is measured by how team members grow in the use of their talents and the new initiatives they undertake.

Successful leaders lead organizations that achieve great things (and make money). That's a positive and, according to some, the only measurement. And If we want to measure the quality of a leader, we look at the success of the organization he or she runs. Whether it's Apple, Facebook, DHL or Netflix, all entrepreneurs look at companies that are super successful and wonder what they do differently. Well, they excel at things that matter the most – and those things against which they and others measure them, whether that's something innovative or offering a better service than anyone else or price or delivery or a combination of all those.

Steve Jobs didn't treat his team with respect. He wasn't a people person and made mistakes with how he managed his employees. What made Steve Jobs legendary was his vision and innovation and that's how he was measured – introducing new products that sold.

A year ago, at the height of their success, Airbnb founder Peter Thiel released an article simply titled, 'Don't F*ck Up the Culture.' He argued that culture was the most important part of the company and that, when a company lives its core values through all aspects of what they do – the less corporate processes a company needs. And that's how he wanted to be measured. Less process, more opportunity, more profit. In 2009, Netflix CEO Reed Hastings put together a massive 124-slide document that has since become legendary, being hailed by Facebook COO Sheryl Sandberg as the "most important document ever to come out of Silicon Valley." This document was called the Netflix Culture Deck and it outlined the Netflix corporate values and hiring strategies. Netflix pays well and honours freedom, trusting employees with a no-questions-asked expenses policy, unlimited vacation time, flexible work schedules, no traditional yearly performance reviews and top-end pay. Its measurement on its activities, and those of its staff, is based on trust.

Richard Branson's tenacity is much admired as is the brand he built. Tenacity has worked for him. His measurement is to try something and see. If it works well, there you go. If not, stop it.

An aspect of measurement, in addition to feedback for continuous improvemnt against agreed KPIs, relates to assumptions. False assumptions are common and can cause problems when the assumptions are a) based on nothing but gut instinct and b) wrong. Gut instinct has a place of course, but over-reliance is dangerous. You also want facts. Also, variables change and if we accurately analyse what's changed and why, we'll have the basis for fixing or developing things. Importantly we'll know better why change has occurred and that's mission critical. Someone unknown said, "You can't manage what you don't measure." True? Probably. Add to that, "If you can't measure it, you can't improve it."

The practice

- Learn what other leaders measure and how. And by the by, the evolving field of analytics is increasingly important.

- Look for a coach or mentor who can focus on measurement – someone who understands measurement and also someone who knows how to bring out the best in you and curb the worst.

- Some neglect measurement because they fear the results. Don't do that. Valuable measurement has everything to do with feedback since it impacts the future. Your organization's and yours.

87

THINK GLOBAL

EVEN IF YOUR ORGANIZATION has only ten staff and is based in Chicago, Barcelona, Bogota or Singapore, it helps your growth to think hard about the world. Not the immediate world alone, but the whole world.

The idea

All successful business leaders have a global understanding – even if they don't operate globally. A global mindset is the ability to perceive behaviours in multiple cultural contexts. It's an ability to connect with and learn from people from other cultures. Leaders who possess a global view are able to view situations from a variety of perspectives and understand a national and international view of relationships and business.

One thing leaders don't do enough is read publications from other parts of the world or engage in international social media – an excellent way to understand how other countries perceive us and which can influence how we behave when we approach new markets. Many countries are way ahead in their use of social media and technology– their expectations are high and opportunities can be high too. It's said that the now global Black Friday got its name because it's the day American retailers get out of the red and into the black for the year. There are equivalents to Black Friday. Imagine the potential growth benefits for a global-minded seller leveraging multiple 'Black Fridays' each year: China has 'Singles Day' (November 11), which in 2017 saw more than 168.2 billion yuan ($25 billion) being spent in 24 hours. Single's Day, promoted annually by Chinese e-commerce giant Alibaba, was supposedly started by bachelor university students in the 1990s who bought themselves presents as a kind of anti-Valentine's day. The retail event is now nearly four times larger than Black Friday and Cyber Monday, the two biggest shopping days in America.

The good news for small businesses looking to enter international markets is that the leap is easier now. PayPal has a free tool for small businesses called PassPort that offers easy to access guidance, country by country. PassPort helps businesses build a checklist of actions to help connections with a localized eCommerce presence. It highlights cultural taboos and trends, identifies seasonal events and sales peaks and specifies tax and customs procedures.

McDonald's used to offer 'one' product worldwide. Now it strives to act on local tastes, e.g. McItaly burger in Italy, Maharaja Mac in India, the McLobster in Canada and the Ebi Filet-O in Japan. Its profits increased big time as a result of ethnic and regional changes. Domestic appliance maker, Whirlpool, incorporated specially designed agitators into its washing machines when it sold them in India. This helped Indian women wash without five-feet long saris getting tangled. Unilever took what it called glocalization (local adaptation) to a new level in the 1990s. Instead of adapting products unnecessarily, it adapted products to the local market marginally i.e. the basic product would be fine-tuned instead of expensive total adaptation. Unilever identified the need for regional differences and was successful, for example, with its Wall's ice cream – adapting it specifically to Asian tastes. One of the most successful tactics of Austrian company Red Bull is to host extreme sports events. From the Red Bull Indianapolis Grand Prix to the Red Bull Air Race in the UK to the Red Bull Soapbox Race in Jordan. And the branding never alters.

Developing a global mindset has to be actively pursued. As we continue to operate on such an interconnected and rapidly changing world stage, the need for globally attuned leaders who are skilled in leading and unifying diversity, will increase.

Regardless of where we work, in whatever industry, the key role of a leader is to influence. To successfully influence in an increasingly multi-cultural world requires understanding, empathy and insight. A growth mindset requires a cosmopolitan outlook, a passion for diversity and a thirst for adventure – as well as understanding, empathy and insight!

The practice

- Understand that the diversity of operating on a global platform brings with it both opportunity and risk.

- Once again, storytelling is vital. You will need to describe what you do and what you offer in different ways to different audiences.

- Look at what stories are rising to the top in Zimbabwe or Vietnam or wherever – they can tell us a lot about what people there are thinking.

- A global presence is possible for any business with a creative strategy, an understanding of world markets, the Internet and social media.

88. LOOK OUT FOR LEADERSHIP TRENDS

THE RAPID PACE OF change is not slowing. Rather, it's the new normal. You should focus on what you can control and influence. But to do that, you need to understand what other people are doing in the name of leadership.

The idea

Trends indicate a change or development in a specific direction. They guide our choices and decisions. Trends point to something that's happening or about to happen. Having the right mindset to absorb trends (and allow them to help us) is important. Ignoring trends can cause us to miss something important.

Permanent customer access will be something that is already focusing many leaders. Customers want what they want when they want it. That will change many business models. Similarly, the way that people work and want to work is already changing. The trend towards virtual offices – remote computing and video meeting capabilities – enables a business to run independently of physical locations. And many businesses will offer and deliver personalized products and services that are customized to a customer's explicit specifications. Risk-taking will be the norm. Intuit is one of the world's largest and most successful financial software companies. Even as a company with nearly $4 billion in revenue and a market cap of approximately $16.5 billion, Intuit continues to operate like a startup. It has a culture where nearly 8,000 employees are allowed/encouraged to take risks and learn from success and failure.

Keeping costs down isn't new, but it's a continual trend and something that focusses the majority of successful businesses and according to

Isaac Perlmutter always will. He was a member of Marvel Comics' board of directors when the company went into bankruptcy in 1996. As the owner of Toy Biz, Inc., he helped merge the company with Marvel to bring it out of bankruptcy in 1998. Focused on licensing for media and products, Marvel improved its cash flow and raised its stock price. Perlmutter, who became Marvel's CEO in 2005, is known for his cost-conscious and low-headcount management. In 2009, Marvel was purchased by Walt Disney for $6 billion.

Quality control and listening to consumers are always facets of business success. Many businesses have rued the time when they reduced quality, size or product scope or didn't match customer expectations. When Toblerone's owner, Mondelez International,reduced the size of the unique chocolate bars: sales diminished. The move had resulted in the weight of the 400g bars being reduced to 360g and the 170g bars to 150g, while the size of the packaging remained the same. Consumer goods giant Unilever fought a brief but furious battle (and lost) with the UK's largest supermarket chain, Tesco Plc over price rises for some of its staples such as Dove deodorant and Marmite.

Another trend that isn't new either, but is gaining prominence amongst many top leaders is employee engagement. Doug Conant became CEO of Campbell's Soup in 2001. Sales were falling due to prior management's decisions to raise prices and the company had lost half its market value. Conant believed the key to success was employee engagement. He replaced 300 of the company's top 350 leaders and implemented a 10-year plan to turn the company around. By 2009, Campbell's stock outperformed the Standard & Poor's Index.

The other main trend is getting the right kind leadership from within a business: smart, agile and digitally savvy leaders who have interdisciplinary skills. Mark Zuckerberg of Facebook has said, "The biggest risk is not taking any risk. In a world that is changing really quickly, the only strategy that is guaranteed to fail is not taking risks." And risk-taking according to Deloitte, "has become one of the most important drivers of a high-performing leadership culture." Millenials take risks. They are the only generation that has grown up completely immersed in technology, so it's only natural that their leadership style will be completely different from the one endorsed by Generation Y. Johnson & Johnson created an affinity group called Millennials to provide leadership opportunities.

There will be issues that will be impossible to escape in terms of aftershocks due mostly to unexpected geopolitical events which will affect trade agreements and the regulatory environment. Then we have rogue states, terrorism and digital theft. New technologies will impact us all and that impact will be beneficial or detrimental. Leadership everywhere in every quarter will need to be strong and as we look around today, can we say that it is?

The practice

- Leaders with a growth mindset are tuned into opportunity solving. That's you.

- Many leaders find it difficult to get comfortable with the virtual world – blogs, vlogs, teleconferencing, Skype, wikis, instant messaging, social networks, video and document-sharing sites, chat boards and so on. Understand them.

- Some say that the solutions for the future aren't found in the past – the trend is to use historical data to influence the creative solutions needed for the future, but not replicate patterns of the past.

THINK LIKE A LEADER

You know that a mindset shift requires you to break away from old behaviours and habits that may no longer be serving you effectively. It demands that you escape your comfort zone and adopt different ways of thinking. Becoming a leader needs similar work and learning. It's also about changing unproductive behaviours and throwing ego away.

The idea

Jack and Suzy Welch wrote in 2013, "Being a leader basically requires a whole new mindset. You're no longer constantly thinking 'How can I stand out?' but 'How can I help my people do their jobs better?' Sometimes that requires undoing a couple of decades of momentum. After all... you've been promoted because someone above you believes you have the stuff to make the leap from star player to successful coach."

One of the core elements of leadership is transparency as we've seen already. That can mean the improvement of everyday practices. If profits suddenly go down, for example, that could be an opportunity to implement change. Coming to a better understanding of the problem might be a team effort but it needs leadership and requires openness and honesty. If information is concealed, temptation grows to manipulate the data to make it look better. Changing our mindset requires us to look at how we engage people, make decisions and evaluate opportunities. And, by the way, it's not the same everywhere so a global outlook is important as we've discussed. Living more in the moment makes India's business leaders very adaptable and opportunistic. Arrive in Mumbai with an idea and no appointments and soon one could be seeing the people at the top. Rarely does this flexibility happen in the West, where lead times are long.

Leadership means accepting (occasional) failure. For example, return-on-investment calculations need to assess results in a way that reflects the agreed-upon objectives, which may have been deliberately designed to include risk. Good leaders can't only plan with models of success. There needs to be a recognition of what happens if some things fail, are less successful or are uncertain. Honda had a recent, dramatic failure. The installation of faulty equipment from its airbag supplier, Takata, led Honda to recall about 8.5 million vehicles. Although the staff accountable were fired, the company also stated that the airbag failure, in itself, was not the problem that led to dismissal. The problem was the lack of attention to the failure at an early stage, when it could have been more easily corrected. The company said, "We forgot that failure is never an acceptable outcome; instead, it is the means to acceptable outcomes."

Another vital leadership trait is that of seeking ideas. McDonald's has terrific innovative skills. This began with the McDonald brothers who applied assembly line methods to hamburger production. They also invented the drive-through restaurant, inspired when a senior executive visited a drive-through bank to drop off a deposit.

Pushing boundaries is similarly key to leadership. Nike has produced hundreds of styles for every kind of foot and activity. The deliberate aim is that they find out what works and what doesn't, not something that all businesses can do of course. Nike reinforces its philosophy by its 'Just Do It' advertising strapline. Others make small tests to make sure their market approves. Coca Cola had a famous 1985 disaster when it misread consumers and brought out what was called New Coke. In the 1970s, baby food business, Gerber, tried to sell adult food (in baby food-style jars). Nobody liked that and the company gave up the idea fast. A leading idea that didn't work and was dropped instantly. Leaders with a growth mindset see opportunities everywhere. Often, they're opportunities that others don't see. Sometimes they don't work.

Most well-known leaders have had a platform on which they established their business. Anita Roddick who founded The Body Shop said, "I want to work for a company that contributes to and is part of the community. I want something not just to invest in. I want something to believe in." Mary Kay Ash founder of Mary Kay cosmetics commented: "People are definitely a company's greatest asset. It doesn't make any difference whether the product is cars or cosmetics. A company is only as good as the people it keeps." And that's core too. A great leader manages his/her people with great communication and engagement. Leaders who listen are able to create trustworthy relationships that are transparent and breed loyalty. Delivering more than anyone ever expects is also a big mindset shift from the ordinary. As Jeffrey Katzenberg wrote, "At DreamWorks, with every movie we make, we start out with the ambition and the goal to exceed the expectations of our audience. We may not succeed every time, and you may not either, but we sure do try."

The practice

- People are looking to you for guidance.

- Unless you're willing to accept that you must take calculated risks sometimes, whatever the consequences, your days in leadership are numbered. Lead knowing that risk is a positive. Then you'll stop being afraid to fail.

- Set big goals that are a stretch, but doable.

- Ask questions and *always* understand the answers.

- Build bridges. Be a connector between the company, the outside world and your teams.

- With a vision in place, you must be able to motivate others to buy in and follow.

HUG THE AGE OF DISRUPTION

A DISRUPTION IS A radical change, necessitating a strategic adjustment often caused by the launch of a new product or service. Or the extension of an existing one. To develop, you must acknowledge disruption and its consequences because disruption can create new opportunities and huge growth.

The idea

We're surrounded by political, social and financial upheavals. We've entered an age of disruptive political surprises, the ultimate consequences and implications of which have yet to unfold.

Disruption has also penetrated every area of industry, causing a rapid acceleration in learning and planning. Amazon's Kindle reader sales were down 69 per cent in 2014 when compared with the year before. However, Amazon had already anticipated this and developed a smartphone app, allowing e-books to be read that way. And it won't be long before wearables – which have only really just come into the market – will be disrupted by 'implantables'. Airbnb has used technology to overturn the hotel industry. It's valued at $25.5 billion, almost $5 billion more than the giant Marriott – not bad, considering it doesn't actually own any property. Online payment provider Alipay started by enabling e-commerce payments in China, but subsequently launched a money market fund that quickly captured one-third of China's 1.46 trillion-yuan market.

Skype, Netflix, Apple and Google rolled out products and services that approached their market in such a unique way that they changed everything. Now there's AI and robotics. The population in space could exceed one trillion people in the 22nd Century. SpaceX, Virgin Galactic, Blue Origin and Stratolaunch Systems are working on space-tourism and colonization funded by billionaires Elon Musk, Richard Branson, Jeff Bezos and Paul Allen respectively. There's 3D printing too and it's possible now to print furniture, utensils, cars, clothes, games, food and body-parts. There are medical innovations that are in existence now that turn health care on its current head including vaccines, genomic directed clinical trials as well as gene and DNA editing.

In his book, *The Innovator's Dilemma*, Clayton Christensen introduced the idea of 'disruptive innovation.' He used this phrase as a way to think about successful companies not just meeting customers' current needs, *but* anticipating their unstated or future needs. Anticipation is a feature of a growth mindset. Christensen explained how small companies with minimal resources were able to enter a market and displace the established system. Tony Robbins, keynote presenter, writes: "Time is going to change your product. I don't care how long it's been around. What used to take glacial periods of time – centuries, the Iron Age, the Ice Age, thousand-year periods of time – started happening in centuries, then started happening in decades and now what's happening? We're doubling the amount of information that man has on the planet, digitized even, every 36 months." He and others maintain that until a leader understands this, all about him/her will change but s/he won't.

The innovation dilemma is the decision an established company faces when it has to choose between hanging onto an existing market by doing the same thing better or capturing markets by adapting something that exists and making it new. IBM approached this by launching a new arm to make PCs, while continuing its mainframe manufacture. Netflix took a radical move leaving its old business model (renting DVDs by post) to a new one (streaming on-demand video to its customers and then making its own movies). Its competitors did none of that.

As successive refinements improve disruptive ideas to the point that they start to steal customers, they may end up reshaping entire industries: classified ads (Craigslist), long distance calls (Skype), record stores (iTunes), research libraries (Google), local stores (eBay), taxis (Uber) and newspapers (Twitter), everything for sale (Amazon).

Tesla is disrupting energy storage with the Tesla Powerwall. Google (on paper an Internet search company), moved into the Android phone business. Android currently commands an 80 per cent market share. Amazon started selling books, but banked on the shift towards e-books. Red Bull (which has sold over 50 billion cans by the way) launched Red Bull Media House to produce original sports and lifestyle content – now a leading premium content media business. Apple is notorious for disruption. In 2001, the company realised there was no quality MP3 player on the market. So, the iPod was developed – selling over 300 million, until the company disrupted its own technology by moving into another adjacent market with the music-playing iPhone. Google and others have invented driverless cars and Amazon promises to reinvent shopping (again) using drones.

The practice

- These are both the best and worst of times. Little is certain. But that shouldn't frighten you. Consider and discuss all the 'what ifs' and create some 'what ifs' of your own.

- Don't be hooked by conspiracy theories.

- Most people have remarkable resources at their fingertips, but never work out how to leverage them.

- Don't be dragged down by excuses, inertia and negative energy. Try something different. You might create new markets; you may discover new categories of customers. That's disruptive change.

CHAPTER 10
DEVELOP AND GROW

BE ENERGETIC

THERE'S NO DOUBTING THE benefits that result when you have the right mindset. But you need to keep it and that needs physical and mental energy.

The idea

It's no good having great goals if there's simply not enough energy to pursue them. The key is to understand how to always maintain a super frame of mind. Well, firstly we decide there's nothing more important than our positive mindset. We can't get entangled with negative interactions that offer no benefit. Wendy Lea, CEO of Get Satisfaction (a community platform for creating engaging customer experiences) shares tips that keep her focused, energized, effective and productive – personally and professionally: "I take fifteen minutes every morning for contemplation and to empty my mind. I take a bag full of thoughts I need cleared and each morning I pick one out, read it and send it down the river near my house. Watching the thought float away really helps clear my mind, reorient things and increase my focus for the rest of the day... I send an email to my team each Monday morning with the top five things I will be focused on for the week. This really keeps me on track and gives me the focus I need."

Anne-Marie Slaugher, a Princeton professor of politics and international relations writes that basing our work day around the never-ending flow of incoming emails is negative – and saps energy. Her, "principal productivity tip is that if you are caught up on your email, your priorities are in the wrong place... Email puts you in response mode, where you are doing what other people want you to do, rather than send mode, where you are deciding what you want to do and taking action."

Equally, positive, creative tension can have a part to play in a company's energy and our own. Christopher Koelsch, CEO of Los Angeles Opera writes, "Don't be afraid of tension and conflict. While it's crucial that a leader should not foment strife, it is equally important to have ballast against conventional wisdom, groupthink and the path of least resistance. This is especially true in the opera house, where creative tension is absolutely essential in creating a product for the audience with maximum musical and theatrical rigor." Energy can equal passion and strength. If we let our passion show to the people we're managing they'll likely become passionate too. Energized leaders are normally effective communicators and their body language reflects their enthusiasm. Energetic leaders look healthy. They eat well and drink water. They exercise regularly.

Interestingly many business leaders believe that passion and mental energy is there or it isn't. Richard Branson in his book, *The Virgin Way: Everything I Know About Leadership*, he writes, "One cannot train someone to be passionate – it's either in their DNA or it's not. Believe me, I have tried and failed on more than one occasion and it cannot be done so don't waste your time and energy trying to light a fire under flame-resistant people. If that basic, smoldering fire is not innate then no amount of stoking is ever going to ignite it."

The practice

- Be passionate about what you do. Passion is the DNA of energy. Passion and energy are also highly contagious.

- If you invest your energy in negative thinking or emotions, then it's a total waste.

- Proper breathing is one of the most important ways to improve your energy level. Try yoga.

- Positive thinking calms irrational thinking by focusing the brain's attention on something that is completely stress free.

- As mentioned earlier, go for walks. Long ones.

- Shift the focus from a problem to its solution.

ROLE MODEL THE BEST PEOPLE

WHETHER WE THINK WE do or don't, we all have people whom we admire for all sorts of things – looks, success, wealth, sporting prowess, strength, achievements of all kinds. Keeping acceptable qualities in mind that we admire in others will keep your growth mindset refreshed and you positive.

The idea

The reasons for attraction are wide. While Steve Jobs may have had his faults, we can't deny that he created a force to be reckoned with. His biggest strengths and most admired abilities were charisma and vision. He didn't sell consumers a product. He sold them an idea that was clean, efficient and appetizing. But a role model doesn't have to be a Steve Jobs. Writes Claudia Zuiderwijk, Chair of KVK (Dutch Chamber of Commerce), "I think role models can be people that are both accessible and doing well, not only mega successful top entrepreneurs. These people should share their disappointments and how they managed to overcome them."

There are a variety of business traits that we might admire. Ingvar Kamprad, founder of IKEA, was heavily criticized because of his reputation for cautious spending, despite his enormous wealth. He famously refused to cut a ribbon to open a building but undid it instead and told the organisers that they could reuse it. If there's a personal standard to admire, we should adopt it if it's relevant to our mindset development – and stick to it no matter what the criticism. Many admire the Virgin Group as a cool brand and Richard Branson as a competitive spirit. The name Ray Kroc is synonymous with persistence in building up McDonald's. He wrote, "Press on; nothing in the world can take the place of persistence. Nothing is more common than unsuccessful men with talent. The world is full of educated derelicts. Persistence and determination alone are omnipotent." We may admire someone like Mohammad Yunus who won the Nobel Peace Prize in 2006 for founding the Grameen Bank which allowed the very poorest in Asia and Africa to get a small loan to build a business where no mainstream banks would help. In business, it's likely to be people who can show vision, motivation, persistence, innovation, communication and leadership.

Successful (and determined) people are conditioned to look forward, to always ask 'what if' and 'why not'. It's that innate curiosity about new things that help those people develop a creative outlook. In 1927, Malcolm Mclean, an American trucker thought, as he watched the contents of his truck being unloaded and then loaded onto a ship, that it would be much faster and convenient if the whole trailer itself were lifted instead. He turned that idea into a reality and that was the start of containerized shipping.

Some innovative ideas take longer and the role model status might be shared depending on what qualities we want or admire. Alexander Fleming discovered penicillin in 1928, but it wasn't until fifteen years later that the drug came into widespread use. Similarly, Alan Turing came up with the idea of a universal computer in 1936, but it wasn't until 1946 that one was actually built – and not until the 1990s that computers began to take off. The reason that Fleming was unable to bring penicillin to market was that, as a biologist, he lacked many of the requisite skills. It wasn't until a decade later that two chemists, Howard Florey and Ernst Boris Chain, picked up the problem and were able to synthesize penicillin. Even then, it took people with additional expertise in fermentation and manufacturing to turn it into the cure we know now. This isn't the exception, but the norm. Darwin's theory of natural selection borrowed ideas from Thomas Malthus, an economist and Charles Lyell, a geologist. Watson and Crick's discovery of DNA was not achieved by only working in a lab, but by incorporating discoveries in biology, chemistry and x-ray diffraction to shape their model building.

Some role models might be extraordinarily modest. Tim Berners-Lee put no patent on his Worldwide Web invention, so was due no royalties. He decided that his invention should be freely available. And some role models might have been clever but not commercial. In 1938, Laszlo Biro patented the ballpoint pen. But having taken out a patent for his invention, he sold it to Marcel Bich in 1945, whose company Bic pocketed the majority of the cash from the 100 billion that have been sold since.

Of course, the obvious role models for most children are our parents, followed by other immediate family and teachers. When we look elsewhere for role models, we have our peers and we have people from films, books, music, sports, business, politics even – and all of these can become a big influence on us and the way we present ourselves. We admire people who handle adversity, health challenges, disabilities well and/or who have an upbeat, optimistic outlook on life.

The practice

- Follow those whom you admire via social media. Learn. It's never copying; it's taking what works for you by getting inspirational input.

- Don't just accept any old stuff that a role model says or does. It may not be right for you.

- Reflect on your strengths and weaknesses. Select an area you don't feel is naturally a strength and find someone who has that strength.

- Whether you admire a pop star, a footballer, a model or a parent, teacher or coach, choose people whose values will work for you.

93 GET OUT OF YOUR COMFORT ZONE AND INTO COMFORT

YOUR COMFORT ZONE IS a space where your activities and behaviours fit a routine that's safe. It provides security. You benefit in obvious ways: comfort, low anxiety and reduced stress. Sometimes, to get away from your comfort zone helps you to achieve and, interestingly, to be happier. Stretching yourself, your beliefs and skills is vital to the reinforcement of a positive mindset.

The idea

Jack Canfield wrote, "The biggest rewards in life are found outside your comfort zone. Live with it. Fear and risk are prerequisites if you want to enjoy a life of success and adventure." Dr Elizabeth Lombardo, therapist and author of *Better Than Perfect*, says people who seek fresh experiences tend to be more creative and emotionally resilient than those who remain stuck in routine. In her view, innovation happens when we step outside our comfort zone. Being stagnant in routine often results in plummeting creativity. "In order to be more creative, we have to try new things, see things in a new way, put pieces together in a new manner," she says. Supporting this, Bear Grylls, the explorer, writes, "Adventure should be 80 per cent 'I think this is manageable,' but it's good to have that last 20 per cent where you're right outside your comfort zone. Still safe, but outside your comfort zone." What holds most of us back from stepping out of our comfort zone, however, is of course fear. "We have such a huge fear of failure in our society," writes Elizabeth Lombardo. Getting comfortable with being uncomfortable is key to overcoming this fear.

The idea of the comfort zone goes back to a psychology experiment in 1908, when psychologists Robert M. Yerkes and John D. Dodson explained that a state of relative comfort created a steady level of performance in order to maximize that performance. However, they said that people need a state of relative anxiety, a space where our stress levels are slightly higher than normal. This space is called optimal anxiety and it's just outside our comfort zone. Too much anxiety and we're over-stressed and can't be productive; our performance drops off sharply.

Anyone who's ever pushed themselves to a next leveling, knows that when they really challenge themselves, they can get amazing results. However, pushing too hard can actually cause a negative result. So, we don't. We get frustrated and walk away in order to return to an anxiety free, comfortable state. But, a growth mindset seeks adventure, experiment and ideas. Pushing boundaries. Reassuringly, none of us can live outside our comfort zones on a permanent basis. We need to 'come back' from time to time to process our experiences and, once absorbed, draw the positive aspects – and act.

The practice

- When was the last time you did something for the first time?

- Now that you have – or are beginning to have – a growth mindset and are positive, you'll find it easier to push your boundaries.

- Don't overdo it. But do it.

- Perfect rarely exists, so stop waiting for perfect. If whatever you're doing fails, then you've simply learnt what didn't work and you're one step closer to what does.

- Push yourself out of your comfort zone to learn what you're really capable of.

WRITE WELL

Mark Twain noted that, "to get the right word in the right place is a rare achievement." He also wrote, "Writing is easy. All you have to do is cross out the wrong words." Writing skills are important in many types of communications including emails, reports, presentations, websites, sales materials, blogs and more. Communication skills are often invariably weak amongst many people, managers included. And that's not good given that mindset growth benefits hugely from clarity of thought and communicating it

The idea

There's a reason Mark Zuckerberg presents Facebook to investors in a hoodie and jeans and why he uses the language of youth in his written communications. It works. In the context of good writing, Lee Iacocca said that, "You can have brilliant ideas, but if you can't get them across, your ideas won't get you anywhere." And much of our time is wasted because of not understanding reading what others have written. Or vice versa. We live in an era of sound-bites and 140 character messages, but good writing still matters when in the business world. Or any world, come to think of it.

People in business must be able to articulate their ideas, instructions, findings, facts and expectations. Michelle Peluso, who's held leadership roles at Travelocity, Citigroup and Gilt, understands that people are motivated by responsive leaders who express themselves well. She, for example, is well known for responding in writing precisely and personally within 24 hours to every e-mail from any employee.

We know that some managers like hand-written notes and letters. Richard Branson recognizes the importance of a handwritten letter, "I find few things make as powerful an impression as the handwritten word. The fact that such a note is not a quick text or email makes it even more outstanding, and valuable. This is why I used to send many handwritten notes in the early days of Virgin, and I still write and mail many letters by hand today."

When a business is able to effectively communicate in clear, simple, yet professional language, such a business will most likely win more customers and have better engaged staff. This is because flawless writing sends signals of simplicity, diligence and quality. Poor writing, on the other hand, quickly destroys a reputation.

Jeff Bezos values writing over talking to such an extreme that in Amazon senior executive meetings, "before any conversation or discussion begins, everyone sits for 30 minutes in total silence, carefully reading six-page printed memos."

Wrote author and aviator Anne Morrow Lindbergh, "Good communication is as stimulating as black coffee, and just as hard to sleep after." Think about that after your next management conference.

The practice

- Write for your audience, not for you – and get to the point.

- You need to know how to write effectively for any purpose. That means paying attention to grammar, spelling and punctuation, along with appropriate word choice and a consistent style.

- Don't let bland corporate-speak creep in to what you write – write in your own voice.

DECISIONS, DECISIONS

You have a choice in almost everything you do. That's important to remember when you're affirming your newly found positivity. Barring a few exceptions, no one holds your feet to the fire on *anything*. There will be choices that we must make – and some we'll get right and some wrong. But we must take responsibility for making and taking choices. A positive mindset will help that happen.

The idea

In *Blink* Malcolm Gladwell wrote, "Great decision makers aren't those who process the most." Many managers will not make a decision and stick with it. This belief, as Gladwell pointed out, can be seen everywhere. When some managers aren't happy with a diagnosis they ask for more data or seek a second opinion.

Sri Sharma, founder and managing director of the search agency Net Media Planet, writes that he has often relied on what he terms his personal radar as he built his company from a single person start-up to a multi-million-pound business. It allowed him to think fast, "Think of your instinct, your gut feeling, as a personal radar that is built up over the years. Often the data you analyse confirms the instinct of your personal radar, but it can't replace it. Instinct is vital."

Jeff Bezos wrote in 2017 that, "Most decisions should probably be made with somewhere around 70 per cent of the information you wish you had. If you wait for 90 per cent, in most cases, you're probably being slow. Plus, either way, you need to be good at quickly recognizing and correcting bad decisions. If you're good at course correcting, being wrong may be less costly than you think, whereas being slow is going to be expensive for sure."

The Dalai Lama once said: "Sometimes not getting what you want is a wonderful stroke of luck." Well, we often think we know what we want and what's right for us. And sometimes we don't. If we think too much about a problem, it's easy to over-complicate and end up more confused than when we started.

Extremely successful people consistently make choices that expand their lives. Jim Collins, author and management consultant, wrote, "Greatness is not a function of circumstance. Greatness, it turns out, is largely a matter of conscious choice." When considering anything relevant to growth mindset development, we don't want to be so ruled by our hearts that all logic disappears. Yet we don't want to only be ruled by the facts (although facts are critical), because gut instinct is strong. But we can be so consumed by the facts that we miss the solutions. It's normal to feel bewildered when different options present different pros and cons. Under the pressure of making the correct choice, all or none of our choices may even seem right.

Ask for advice from others, but remember that people are naturally biased (and flawed as are we all) because they're dealing with their own dilemmas. Anyone can offer you their take on what's right, but few can offer you what's right for *you*; by and large only you can do that.

The practice

- Positive thoughts lead to possibilities.

- When facing a dilemma, structure your thinking but don't always over-analyze.

- Keep a balance between your head and your heart; don't throw logic out.

- It's important to listen to others and also your intuition.

- Making good choices begins with taking charge of the decision-making process.

- Do your best to act for the good of everyone, not just for your own good. When in doubt, consult your moral code.

CONSIDER WHAT ADVICE YOU GIVE TO PEOPLE

SHARE YOUR EXPERIENCE WITH your teams, colleagues and direct reports – not in a hectoring or arrogant (I've done it all) kind of way, but in a proactive, example-driven, helpful and supportive way that is fit for purpose. What you say may not resonate and may not be valid (to the recipients), so you have to choose when to give vent, And, as importantly, how.

The idea

Kevin Johnson, Starbucks' CEO, is working hard to grow the chain from 26,000 locations today to 37,000 by 2021 – while maintaining the brand's appeal. His guiding principle is to be authentic. That's the advice he gives his people – by acknowledging shortcomings and weaknesses we allow ourselves and the people around us to do their best work. Berkshire Hathaway Warren Buffett, with a worth of $73 billion, writes that the best advice a leader can give is to tell people to take on a job or do work that makes them excited each day. PepsiCo's CEO Indra Nooyi says that the best advice she would give is that people should deliver the hard not just the easy, "Nobody notices when you do an easy job well. It's far better to challenge yourself... and solve problems that no one else has been able to solve." Marissa Mayer, former CEO of Yahoo, would counsel her younger self to get comfortable with being uncomfortable (something we've discussed) and taking on tasks that we think we might not be fully prepared for. She explains, "I always did something I was a little not ready to do."

Most advice and the stories in which that advice is embedded must inspire and can't just be a showing off device. Richard Branson agrees with that. He, incidentally, advises his people on the following theme,

"My mother always taught me never to look back in regret but to move on to the next thing." Maureen Chiquet, Global CEO, Chanel was told by Mickey Drexler, once CEO of Gap, "I'm going to give you some important advice. You're a terrific merchant. But you've gotta learn to listen!" And Shafqat Islam, CEO and co-founder, Newscred says, "If you're not getting told 'no' enough times a day, you're probably not doing it right or you're probably not pushing yourself hard enough."

Brian Chesky, co-founder of Airbnb was told by Paul Graham who co-established start-up consultancy Y Combinator, "Build something 100 people love, not something 1 million people kind of like." And one can't disagree much with that.

The practice

- No matter what industry or type of business you're in, learning from the experiences of successful leaders can help you not only avoid critical mistakes, but also make informed decisions to help your business grow.

- Listen to others before telling them your view.

- You might consider these questions before offering advice, "What's the idea?" "How are we going to achieve it?" "What is my role?"

- Offer advice that is meaningful and relevant and that is useful for the recipient. Obvious? You'd think so.

97 KEEP YOUR GLASS HALF FULL

We can't always be 100 per cent positive 24/7. It's not possible, but we can look at what we do more positively than negatively and you must, otherwise you can't achieve or succeed.

The idea

You don't, but some people do, think in a distorted way about maintaining positivity, e.g. "Nothing ever works out for me." They inevitably won't invest in their mindset with confidence. When times are tough personally or professionally, many people struggle to stay optimistic. But, just because we *find* reasons for feeling pessimistic doesn't mean that we always should. The fact is, optimism creates opportunity and pessimism kills it.

Positive thinking can set us up for success in every area of our lives. It doesn't guarantee it, but it is a platform. PepsiCo's Indra Nooyi, has written, "Whatever anybody says or does, assume positive intent." Her thinking is that when people have negative intent, they're usually angry or frustrated. If they can change that, they'll be able to do things better. Interestingly, in 2015 and in-line with positive over negative, PepsiCo began producing healthier snacks and drinks.

Estée Lauder, although she didn't know, was a proponent of growth mindset development. She wrote, "Projecting your mind into a successful situation is the most powerful means to achieve goals." And Sakichi Toyoda, of Toyota fame, said, "Before you say you can't do something, try it." Mary Kay Ash founded her "dream business," Mary Kay Cosmetics, after she retired, which proves it's *never* too late to accomplish our goals. Ash's business philosophy was always, "If you think you can, you can. And if you think you can't, you're right."

A positive attitude causes positive events and outcomes. Not always, but often. It's a catalyst. A good way of putting it comes from philanthropist W. Clement Stone, "There is little difference in people but that little difference makes a big difference. The little difference is attitude. The big difference is whether it is positive or negative." *Expecting* good things to happen will lead to taking actions that produce positive results. Howard Schultz made sure all 190,000 Starbucks employees were well aware that the Asian markets had collapsed in 2015. In a compelling memo, he encouraged staff to show special consideration to consumers in the region: "Our customers are likely to experience an increased level of anxiety and concern. Please recognize this and – as you always have – remember that our success is not an entitlement, but something we need to earn, every day. Let's be very sensitive to the pressures our customers may be feeling, and do everything we can to individually and collectively exceed their expectations." Problems come our way all the time. Some are opportunities. This is a good line from Lebanese writer, Kahlil Gibran: "The optimist sees the rose and not its thorns; the pessimist stares at the thorns, oblivious of the rose."

The practice

- The word 'optimism' actually derives from the Latin word 'optima,' meaning the best outcome or belief in the greatest good.

- Optimists are more productive, easier to work with and are more resilient.

- Before you get out of bed take a minute to set your intention for the day. Say it out loud. Being intentional acts like a compass and helps you better focus your energy.

- Optimism is contagious. So too is pessimism.

98 | BECOME SUPER MOTIVATED

WE ALL STRUGGLE WITH motivation. At times, it can feel like we have motivation in spades to be active, to do things and to do yet more things – and to do them all well. At other times, motivation to do things feels as elusive as a grail. With your mindset in a good state, the first option has to be prevalent for you. Remember, motivation is an option.

The idea

Internal motivation is basically when we do something because we find it enjoyable. External motivation is when you do something for external rewards – or to avoid negative consequences. We all know deep down that any level of success depends on our commitment (and push to achieve) goals and sticking with a plan that works. There is a saying: "If you fail to plan, you plan to fail." When you take time to plan, you allow yourself to think through the entire process from beginning to end. And that sparks motivation. Motivation isn't magic. It's about super positivity and a can-do attitude knowing that what's at the end of the process is worth having. Winston Churchill famously said this during London's toughest times in World War II, "Never, ever, ever, ever, ever, ever, ever, give up."

The faster we move, the better we get in trying to achieve something. And the better we get, the more we like ourselves. And the more we like ourselves the higher our self-esteem. And the higher our self-esteem the greater our self-discipline. And so on. Daniel Lubetzky, CEO of Kind Healthy Snacks, writes, "You can't get everybody to give the best of themselves unless you understand what drives each individual and what they care about the most." And Richard Branson adds, "Once you know what your own motivations and aspirations are, you should encourage your employees and colleagues to discover theirs – and then structure their jobs in a way that allows them to tap into that energy too."

The most inspirational managers ignite a spark within their people that get them to act. Their people become inspired too. That's important and inspiration comes from within and also from terrific communication from the top. Communication has to be the platform for superb motivation come what may.

The practice

- It's likely that you have people who see you as leader and, if *you're* not motivated, then sure as hell they won't be.

- Look at some great and inspirational speeches e.g. J.K. Rowling: *The Fringe Benefits of Failure, and the Importance of Imagination* (2008), Steve Jobs: *How to Live Before You Die* (2005) or almost any of Barack Obama's.

- Some things are within your control, while others are not. Learn to recognize the difference.

- Focusing on your strong points every day will forge a powerful sense of self, which will lead to dramatically higher motivation.

- Motivation pushes you to accomplish a task, or work through a difficult event, even when you would rather be doing anything else.

KEEP FIT

SOME EXERCISE HAS MASSES of benefit for you, but be clear on the reason why you're exercising. Is it to lose weight, set a good example to your children, feel fitter, run a race, improve your cholesterol and blood pressure, reduce stress? Keep these reasons in mind whenever you want to sprawl on the couch. Use the power of affirmations to change the way you think and to then reinforce the changes you've made.

The idea

Staying in shape can make us smarter. "Memory retention and learning functions are all about brain cells actually changing, growing and working better together," says John J. Ratey, clinical associate professor of psychiatry at Harvard Medical School and the author of *Spark: The Revolutionary New Science of Exercise and the Brain.* "Exercise creates the best environment for that process to occur," he writes.

Exercise pumps more blood throughout the body, including to the brain. More blood means more oxygen and, therefore, better-nourished brain tissue. Exercise helps the brain to produce more of a protein called brain-derived neurotrophic factor, or BDNF. This powerful protein encourages brain cells to grow and interconnect. Craig Esrael, CEO of First South Financial, remembers enduring cruel teasing as an obese child. He began turning his life around as a teenager, losing 65 pounds in one summer, and remains committed to fitness today. In the workplace he provides healthy foods, exercise and yoga programmes. Esther Dyson, EDventure Holdings' chair, swims and cycles each day. "I don't know much about meditation, but I suspect that this daily routine – more mental than physical – has kept me sane and balanced."

Anna Wintour, editor in chief of *Vogue*, plays tennis each day before heading into work. Mark Holowesko, founder and CEO of Holowesko Partners, often cycles up to 80 miles per day, and swims during his lunch hour. Congresswoman Nancy Pelosi plans her day during her 45-minute morning power walks. "Staying in shape is very important," writes Mark Zuckerberg on Facebook about his workout habits. "Doing anything well requires energy, and you just have a lot more energy when you're fit." ConocoPhillips caters to employees differently throughout the world. In Norway, for example, they have a biking group to train for the grueling, annual Nordsjøritt (North Sea Ride) from Egersund to Stavanger.

The practice

- Exercise doesn't have to be formal. Run up and down your stairs 10 times a day.

- Close your eyes and visualize yourself exercising and how good you'll feel.

- Before you actually begin your new workout routine, set a goal for yourself.

- If you're considering joining a gym, many gyms have personal trainers available to help you set a goal for yourself.

- As physical as exercise is, the first step to any kind of exercise is your mental state. It's important to remember that you exercise, not to torture yourself, but to make yourself feel good.

STAND ON THE SHOULDERS OF GIANTS

"IF I HAVE SEEN further, it is by standing upon the shoulders of giants." wrote Isaac Newton. This is all about learning, adding value to what you know, incorporating what you know with that of the achievements of others, to make you better at whatever you are and want to be.

The idea

The above quote is from a letter written to fellow scientist, Robert Hooke in February 1675. The phrase is understood to mean that, if Newton had been able to discover more about the universe than others, then it was because he was working in the light of discoveries made by fellow scientists. In principle, we'd all like that, no matter on what we're working.

Stephen Hawking's compilation of works by the greatest minds is called *On The Shoulders of Giants: The Great Works of Physics and Astronomy*. When you look at iconic leaders and entrepreneurs, it's easy to focus on the outward symbols of their success – money, respect, acquisitions. Yet it's their internal achievement, the development of a growth mindset, that's really their greatest driver of success.

There is a common misconception that we have to do everything all by ourselves and that everything in life is always up to us. But we learn from the wisdom of others and, while that's simple logic, it's rarely applied.

Also information from other backgrounds or experiences will be a source of inspiration that will broaden your perspective. Exposure to any new and valid experiences (and people) will add value to what you are – or are becoming.

Time spent alone helps reinforce your mindset too. It allows us to think about 'giants' – and don't forget that your 'Giants can be anyone who has ideas that work for you.

No one has everything about mindset generation and reinforcement all worked out, but there are people (some you know and some you don't) who can offer wisdom and advice.

The most successful entrepreneurs and leaders live with a growth mindset and they view learning as a necessary and regular activity that contributes to their personal growth and professional success. People with a growth mindset try new challenges, take qualified risks and use effort as a path to mastering something. They learn from others and stand on their shoulders to do it. If those shoulders belong to giants, then they probably won't mind.

The practice

- Meet others who have skills, knowledge and experiences that differ from your own. If you don't already, start meeting high performers in other industries or professions.

- It's easy to fall into the trap of thinking that you don't have enough time to learn, but that's simply not true. We all have the same amount of time in our days.

- Find books that feed your curiosities. Reading provides new knowledge, fresh perspectives and a playful imagination that can carry over into all parts of our lives. Ditto good blogs and podcasts.

- Learn from best practice. Junior people have as many good practices as seniors.

- Your mindset has to grow and you have to be positive. And to make that happen you have to begin. If that means standing on giants' shoulders for a while, then do it.

"If this book has a lesson, it is that we are awfully lucky
to be here – and by 'we' I mean every living thing.
To attain any kind of life in this universe of ours appears
to be quite an achievement. As humans we are doubly lucky,
of course: We enjoy not only the privilege of existence but also
the singular ability to appreciate it and even, in a multitude of ways,
to make it better. It is a talent we have only barely begun to grasp."

– Bill Bryson, *A Short History of Nearly Everything*

ABOUT THE AUTHOR

 Simon Maier is a prolific author on a variety of themes: communications, the power of oratory, the event management industry, evil and abuse at work as well as amazing historical moments. Some of his books are serious and journalistic, while others are comedic and fun. All are insightful.

Simon has lectured in Shakespeare in the UK and the U.S., managed international communication agencies and has delivered some famous, global events. He regularly presents on digital disruption and mindset growth as well as on communication breakdown, leadership and the future of work.

This book was written because he sees and has seen huge benefit in people in all walks of life changing from a fixed to a growth mindset and the results have been extraordinary. Staying on top of our world of uncertainty is as much about planning for failure as it is about hoping for the best. There is also a Bernard Shaw quote that drove this book: "Life isn't about finding yourself. Life is about creating yourself." And it's positivity like that which encourages Simon to tackle subjects that many others won't.

Simon is passionate about theatre and has directed a number of plays. He lives in Suffolk in the UK and has a dog called Frankie.